THE APP ECONOMY

Making Sense of Platform
Power in the Age of AI

Konrad Kollnig

I0011273

BRISTOL
UNIVERSITY
PRESS

First published in Great Britain in 2026 by

Bristol University Press
University of Bristol
1–9 Old Park Hill
Bristol
BS2 8BB
UK
t: +44 (0)117 374 6645
e: bup-info@bristol.ac.uk

Details of international sales and distribution partners are available at bristoluniversitypress.co.uk

DOI: 10.51952/9781529247725

British Library Cataloguing in Publication Data
A catalogue record for this book is available from the British Library

ISBN 978-1-5292-4770-1 paperback
ISBN 978-1-5292-4771-8 ePub
ISBN 978-1-5292-4772-5 OA PDF

Cover design: Andy Ward
Front cover image: Stocksy/Sibila and Pavel

From KK to CK. May our hearts forever
be united.

Contents

List of Figures

About the Author

Konrad Kollnig holds a PhD in Computer Science from the University of Oxford. This research was awarded the Council of Europe's Rodotà Award of 2024, the highest award for PhD theses in privacy law. This book builds on this PhD research and goes beyond privacy, and caters to everyone who wants to learn about the app economy in depth. It is driven by the question: how do Apple and Google use their dominance in the app economy for their bottom line, with what consequences for society, and how to respond? Konrad Kollnig has developed apps since 2009, when the app economy was still in its infancy. In particular, he created the TrackerControl app, a privacy technology that is used by millions of Android users every day.

Acknowledgements

I thank Jeremias Adams-Prassl and Carissa Véliz for encouraging me to write a book in the first place and helping me navigate the process. I thank Aurelia Tamò-Larrieux and Gijs van Dijck for helping me make Maastricht and legal research my second home. I thank Siddhartha Datta for his continuous inspiration and support; thanks to him, the research in my PhD and beyond has always reliably been delightful.

I thank Theo Hickfang, Talha Paracha, Constanța Roșca, and Thomas Șerban von Davier for their helpful comments on earlier versions of the manuscript. I thank the staff of Bristol University Press for supporting me in making this book available. In addition, I thank the anonymous reviewers who have helped improve this manuscript significantly.

I am grateful for the funding provided by UK Research and Innovation to make this book available via open access. It emerged from my DPhil research at the University of Oxford, which was funded by the UK Engineering and Physical Sciences Research Council under grant number EP/R513295/1.

Finally, I thank Connor Daniel Scott Kirkpatrick for being my best friend for 7.5 years until his sudden death at age 30 in May 2024. Although he experienced more than most of us could ever imagine or bear, he was always my compass, even in the darkest hours, particularly when I was starting to lose hope during the COVID-19 pandemic. In light of this, I wish to donate all of my humble proceeds from publishing this book to Mind, a UK charity for mental health.

Introduction: Welcome the Rulers of the App Economy

Two new powerful actors are among us, but have you noticed? And what risks may they bring? These actors are daily companions of most of us and track every step of our lives; however, they are not authoritarian governments. They operate some of the largest workforces that moderate online discourse; however, they are not social networks, and they have created some of the most successful and manipulative entertainment systems, and they are not game studios. This is all to sell digital ads, content and devices.

It started in 2007 with the launch of the first iPhone. With this device, Steve Jobs, the co-founder and then Chief Executive Officer (CEO) of Apple, promised a new device that combined a phone, an iPod music player, and a web browser. Apple did not invent the smartphone; however, they did substantially improve it. The smartphone market had been around for a few years and was dominated by several firms, including BlackBerry, Palm, and Nokia. However, these incumbents failed to innovate, especially to move to convenient multi touch screens and build a competitive and accessible app economy (Competition and Markets Authority, 2022b).

Interestingly, the highly successful App Store was only added in July 2008, approximately 1.5 years after the release of the first iPhone. It featured an initial selection of 500 apps. Introducing a centralised location for users to download third-party apps was a game-changer for the mobile industry. Google quickly copied the concept, and launched the Android Market (now rebranded Google Play Store) in October 2008. Today, there are approximately 2 million iOS apps and another 2 million in the Google Play Store. In 2021 alone, the two app stores generated over $130 billion in revenue for developers (Business of Apps, 2021). Apps have become a gigantic business. The average American now spends about 5 hours daily with their phone, and checks it every 5–10 minutes; similar trends occur in many other parts of the world.

The influence that Apple and Google hold in our daily lives through their app ecosystems (iOS and Android) is immense because they set the rules and standards for millions of apps and devices that are relied on for communication, entertainment, and more. Their impact is felt globally, and finding an area of life that remains untouched by their influence is challenging. However, the risks resulting from the concentration of power with Apple and Google have rarely been holistically studied before. This is one of the things that this book sets out to address.

1.1 Who's the rule maker and taker?

One of the most prominent displays of the increasing power of Apple and Google over society was during the COVID-19 pandemic. When the pandemic first broke out, many experts placed high hopes on contact tracing apps as a countermeasure. Among them was the team of Carmela Troncoso and Marcel Salathé at the Swiss Federal Institute of Technology Lausanne (EPFL), which hosts one of Europe's most renowned computer science faculties. These contact tracing apps promised to allow us to track contacts easily so that infection chains could be stopped and, therefore, the virus. These efforts did not accomplish the wished-for results (although there were some positive effects on pandemic prevention) (AlgorithmWatch, 2021). The decisions by Apple and Google played a role in this.

Contact tracing apps could only be deployed with the help of Apple and Google, and according to their rules. In April 2020, Apple and Google collaborated in an unprecedented way to implement a privacy preserving, decentralised contract tracing framework that would work across Android and iOS (Exposure Notification). This collaboration required the two companies to overcome their long-standing rivalry in the smartphone market and join forces for the common good: population health. In Apple and Google's Exposure Notification framework, smartphones use Bluetooth signals to exchange an identifier with all nearby participating smartphones. This identifier changes every 15–20 minutes to protect user privacy. Then, all participating phones keep track of what identifiers they saw and when. In a confirmed infection, an individual could upload their observed identifiers and thereby notify other potentially infected individuals. No location or other personally identifiable data was ever shared with third parties. This is the 'decentralised' approach to digital contact tracing.

The design of the Exposure Notification technology was based on a design developed by Professors Carmela Troncoso and Marcel Salathé from EPFL and various other researchers, which they called the Decentralized Privacy-Preserving Proximity Tracing (DP3T). At lightning speed, these researchers developed this technology. In April 2020, Professor Salathé commented 'I've made a few correct predictions about Covid, in a tweet. 'But I would not in a 100 years have predicted this: US tech companies provide a privacy-preserving framework to do digital contact tracing, and some European countries are lobbying them to lower the standards' (CNBC, 2020).

In addition, early in the pandemic, many governments were working on alternative contact tracing technologies, some of which might have given authorities more insights into the identities of infected individuals and their close contacts. However, those approaches would have relied on the storage of personal data on a central server. Developing such centralised and more insightful solutions quickly proved impossible because Apple's iOS operating system would not allow apps to run continuously in the background and track user activity. Therefore, Germany, Australia, and the UK had to cancel their initial plans for such an app (Leprince-Ringuet, 2020; TechCrunch, 2020b; *The Guardian*, 2020). Indeed, the UK had already developed a prototype of its system and conducted a test on the Isle of Wight in May 2020 (Leprince-Ringuet, 2020). In addition, Apple refused France's request to make the necessary changes to iOS to deploy its contact tracing app (Lero, 2022).

The two companies argued that they developed and deployed the technology in the interest of public health while protecting citizens' privacy and limiting potential government overreach based on the sensitive data collected. These concerns have largely not come true, albeit with some exceptions (Amnesty International, 2020; ABC, 2021; NPR, 2021; Reuters, 2021, 2022). Could we have tackled the pandemic more effectively had we not followed the decisions of Google and Apple and opted for a different design of contact tracing? Might a considerable number of lives have been spared? In addition, shouldn't it be democratically elected governments that ultimately decide on the rules of their society, especially in times of crisis? After all, Apple and Google, by law, are foremost committed to their shareholders and not public offices or the electorate.

1.2 Where's the harm?

The rise of these actors falls into a time in which everyday citizens feel like they are losing representation and a say in the democratic process, including the ability to make meaningful decisions about how society works at large. There are many reasons why this is the case.

One is a growing divide between the precariat (Standing, 2016) and an unelected technical elite in Silicon Valley that makes decisions that affect us all. A few reap enormous and disproportionate profits and power from their operations (Competition and Markets Authority, 2020; 2022b), which is best demonstrated by Elon Musk's rise to the White House following Donald Trump's re-election. In doing so, Silicon Valley innovators help to replace existing work with more precarious working conditions (for example, Uber in the taxi industry) and have profoundly changed many existing professions (for example, Google in advertising). Instead of giving back to their communities to the same extent as other companies, these large tech companies often profit from lucrative tax loopholes. Anyone who has walked along the streets of San Francisco has visibly seen some of the problems that result from extracting vast profits but not giving back to their communities sufficiently. Issues such as homelessness and drug abuse are in plain sight. This is despite San Francisco being one of the wealthiest US cities and having a gross domestic product (GDP) of nearly $300,000 per capita, more than four times the US average.

To obtain their enormous profits, tech companies exploit loopholes in the tax systems and kneecap competition in digital markets. For example, Apple paid an effective corporate tax rate of 0.005 per cent in 2014 in the European Union (EU) (European Commission, 2016). Google pays up to 9 per cent of its revenue in taxes outside of the EU; this ratio was about 0.8 per cent inside the EU between 2013 and 2015 (Reuters, 2017). Some of these tax practices might not be illegal, although there is reason to believe that some might be. In October 2023, the Internal Revenue Service (IRS, the US tax authority) asked Microsoft for a record $28.9 billion in back taxes, interest, and penalties over its attempts to funnel profits through Puerto Rico (Windows Central, 2023). Meanwhile, in the EU, there have been long-running legal disputes between the European Commission and Ireland, which is known as a tax haven for tech companies within the EU.

Another reason is that the electoral process is increasingly driven by social media, which is mainly used via smartphones. For example, 82 per cent of Facebook users worldwide exclusively access Facebook via their mobile phones (Statista, 2022a). This is the same social network that caused the Cambridge Analytica scandal (through which Meta or Facebook contributed to the Brexit and 2016 Trump campaigns) and played a 'determining role' (Reuters, 2018) in the mass murder of the Rohingya Muslims in Myanmar. The design of mobile app ecosystems by Apple and Google, helping make phones highly engaging and profit driven, has played a role in this. After all, Apple and Google take up to 30 per cent commission on transactions made via their respective app stores, which creates strong incentives to increase time spent with digital content. For example, how often have you checked your phone for the current time, just to find yourself scrolling for an hour through your Instagram feed? Right now, there is no way to turn off the time being shown on the lock screen on Android or iOS, which limits the extent to which one might be drawn into bad phone habits.

The underlying designs of these app ecosystems are deliberate and driven by the bottom line of the governing tech companies. At the heart of the app economy is the wish to make revenue from device sales (Apple), online ads (Google), and commissions on app store transactions (Apple and Google). All three require detailed knowledge of the users of the technology (to sell more devices, ads, and app content) and, therefore, come with large-scale data collection about user behaviours on their smartphones (tracking).

Regarding tracking, the immediate harms that arise from it vary and are highly individual. They include threats to individuals as much as threats to society as a whole. Individuals often have no real choice over their data (for example, in the absence of consent banners or when manipulative user elements (dark patterns) are used) (Gray et al, 2018; Nouwens et al, 2020; Kollnig et al, 2021a). When given a choice, this is often ineffective (for example, when consent banners assume user consent regardless of a user's choice (Matte et al, 2019). In addition, individuals are often not fully aware of the consequences of their choices over data (McDonald and Cranor, 2008; Shklovski et al, 2014). Tracking within apps underpins many artificial intelligence (AI)-driven technologies, including recommender systems, online behavioural advertising, and political micro targeting. It has been shown that they could lead to a polarisation of online discourse on social media, threaten the integrity of elections, discriminate against disadvantaged groups (for example, making them miss out on attractive jobs and other offers), and help design highly addictive and distracting technologies (Wachter, 2019a; Lyngs et al, 2020). In general, many individuals feel that they have lost control over their data and privacy, leading to frustration and resignation regarding the design of fundamental digital technologies in the 21st century (Shklovski et al, 2014; Colnago et al, 2020; Lyngs et al, 2020).

1.3 The importance of systemic risks

In response to some of these concerns, legislators and policy makers worldwide are debating the right course of action. One response, pursued by the Organisation for Economic Co-operation and Development (OECD) and G20, is introducing a global minimum tax rate of 15 per cent on corporate profits. This aims to put an end to large companies pitting countries against each other in the race to secure ultra low rates (OECD, 2023) and funnel revenues through tax havens, such as the Cayman Islands, Ireland, and the US (*Washington Post*, 2016; Sadek, 2022).

Another response is a set of legal initiatives aimed at the digital ecosystem. The EU has been one of the leaders in many ways. The first step was the introduction of the General Data Protection Regulation (GDPR) in 2016, which seeks to facilitate the flow of data across the EU while protecting individuals' fundamental rights and freedoms (including privacy and data protection). The GDPR has caused much controversy, because its introduction prompted a significant increase in (often meaningless (Matte et al, 2019; Nouwens et al, 2020)) cookie banners, to the annoyance of online users. However, contrary to widespread industry lobbying, cookie notices were not imposed by the GDPR. The term cookie isn't mentioned once in the main text of the GDPR; it was introduced by the 2002 EU ePrivacy Directive. Instead, the GDPR brought potentially significantly higher fines (up to 4 per cent of a company's global annual turnover), which suddenly made companies care much more about their compliance with these laws.

Cookie notices, according to the 2002 EU law, often do not comply with the actual legal requirements (nor mandated as such), and enforcement has been slow. As my previous research found (Kollnig et al, 2021a), among the Android apps on the Google Play Store, most (more than 70 per cent) immediately start sharing data with third-party tracking companies, such as Facebook and Google, when opening these apps for the first time. Of note, at this point, no user has been able to accept any data practices, although this is usually required before tracking under the 2002 EU law. Further inspection of these apps showed that less than 3.3 per cent of the apps implemented consent in a way that fulfils the minimum requirements for tracking under EU law.

More recently, in recognition of the societal risks online platforms pose, the EU has been moving to tackle them directly. Therefore, in late 2022, the EU adopted two new laws: (1) the Digital Markets Act (DMA); and (2) the Digital Services Act (DSA). These laws, as well as their implications and shortcomings, will be discussed later in this book, particularly Chapter 4 on the legal framework. As an analytical lens for the rest of this book, the DSA introduces an important concept: 'systemic risks'. With this term, the DSA acknowledges that online platforms, such as the app ecosystems developed by Apple and Google, play a central role in safeguarding democracy. In response, the DSA contains many measures to help address these systemic risks. These include the need for platforms to file annual reports about their measures against systemic risks and to give researchers access to data to study these risks.

The DSA defines four broad categories of systemic risks (in Article 34): (1) the dissemination of illegal content through their services; (2) negative effects on the exercise of fundamental rights (particularly privacy); (3) negative effects on civic discourse, elections, and public security; and (4) negative effects on gender-based violence, public health (including people's mental well-being), and the protection of minors.

The DSA applies to app ecosystems; the text of the law makes it rather apparent that it was not primarily written with app ecosystems in mind but instead at social media platforms, such as Facebook and Twitter. This is highlighted by the fact that much of the DSA deals with illegal content and misinformation, including content moderation. However, these are not usually the primary issues that arise from the design of app ecosystems by Apple and Google, because these companies only indirectly affect content moderation on social media. Analogous observations are valid for the DMA, the DSA's close relation. This book will discuss these aspects in more detail.

An important reason for the lack of more explicit regulation of app ecosystems is that most previous research and public debate on platforms did not cover app stores. Most of the previous work derives from media and communication studies, focusing on social media companies (Ajunwa and Greene, 2019) and not app stores. If app stores are mentioned, they are often only in a footnote (Srnicek, 2016).

The most extensive coverage of app stores in previous research can be found in *Platforms and Cultural Production* (Poell et al, 2022). In their book, the authors examine the influence of platformisation on cultural production and the processes behind it. The authors discuss in detail how Apple and Google's content policies and moderation affect those seeking to produce and distribute apps. However, the authors rarely go beyond content policies and moderation and, as such, seem to focus mainly on similarities between app stores and other platforms rather than what makes them unique and might motivate a more targeted and nuanced regulation of them.

1.4 Method and approach

Much has been said about the impact of specific types of apps, such as social media or ride hailing, on society. This is not the focus of this book. Neither does this book aim to blame Apple and Google for the adverse effects of the app economy. There have been innumerable positive effects, which is why citizens embraced and adopted smartphones so quickly. There are now approximately 2 million different publishers of mobile apps (42matters, 2023) and more than 6 billion smartphone users (Statista, 2024). In the UK, 'consumers are willing to spend substantial sums of money on them (equivalent to almost £500 per household in 2021)' (Competition and Markets Authority, 2022a).

Despite the high societal relevance of the app economy, most previous research and public debate on online platforms has been on social media and e-commerce, not app ecosystems. Where there is discussion about or regulation of the app economy, these are driven by economic interests and companies with large budgets for lawsuits and lobbying. For example, Spotify, Epic Games (the owner and developer of Fortnite), or Match Group (the owner of Tinder, OkCupid, and Hinge) have been pushing strongly against Apple taking a 30 per cent commission on all app store transactions. Broader societal risks that arise from app store power, including risks to freedom of speech, data protection, privacy, and personal autonomy, have rarely been holistically studied across the app economy. This book attempts to change this by focusing on how (technical) decisions by Apple and Google in the app economy might pose 'systemic risks.' Therefore, this book does not principally focus on the DSA. Instead, this book uses the DSA's concept of 'systemic risk' as a lens to guide its analysis, move beyond immediate financial discussion, and focus on how those without a strong lobby are affected by the decisions taken by Apple and Google in the app economy: citizens such as you and me.

In addition, this book seeks to highlight how the app economy gives Apple and Google a competitive advantage in other sectors, including AI, healthcare, defence, electric vehicles, and others. Based on this, this book develops a framework to understand Apple and Google's influence on society and makes suggestions on how we as a society, including academics, policy makers, non-governmental organisations (NGOs), and citizens, could respond.

This book will sometimes use the word 'power', but mainly uses it in the sense of market dominance under competition law. In the words of the UK competition authority, 'Apple and Google have a tight grip over these increasingly crucial [mobile app] ecosystems – putting them in a powerful position. Both companies unilaterally determine the 'rules of the game'. These problems are entrenched and will not go away unless steps are taken' (Competition and Markets Authority, 2022a). For geographical scope, this book mainly focuses on Europe. In addition, China and the US will be discussed to some extent, given the global relevance of Apple and Google's app ecosystems. For simplicity, Apple's iPads will be seen as smartphones running iOS in this book (because the software and hardware are almost the same as in iPhones).

In addition, what makes this book stand out from other research might be its most significant limitation. The author (even now working as a law professor at a law faculty internationally renowned for its expertise in EU law) holds degrees in computer science rather than social sciences or law. As such, the analysis in this book will be driven less by looking at the laws and theories but rather by trying to make sense of the technical underpinnings of the app economies and how explicit (technical) decisions by Apple and Google affect fundamental rights and freedoms. In addition, this book differs from other research on online platforms and strives to equip the reader with unique perspectives on the technical and non-technical aspects of the app economy. However, this book's readership is intentionally chosen to be non-technical. Therefore, the book has a whole chapter that explains the technical foundations of the app economy. Having developed TrackerControl, a popular privacy app for Android with more than 200,000 downloads, the author has a bias towards privacy and data collection in apps.

1.5 Structure of this book

The rest of the book is structured into three parts: (I) Foundations; (II) Risks; and (III) Conclusions. Chapters 2–5 cover the foundations of the app economy, including key concepts, a historical overview, the legal framework for app store providers, and technical and legal research methods. Chapters 6–9 zoom in on different risks emerging from the app economy and how these are linked to decisions taken by Apple and Google. Finally, Chapters 10–12 provide a framework to discuss Apple and Google's platform power in the app economy and make suggestions on how to respond.

Specifically, Chapter 2 discusses the foundations of the app economy. This might well be one of the most essential elements of this book, trying to equip the reader with the most important technical knowledge to navigate mobile app technology. Chapter 3 gives a brief history of the app economy. It starts from the pre-smartphone era and moves all the way to the present. In particular, right now, we are seeing the rise of a new wave of AI tools, particularly AI models and digital assistants. The winners and losers in the AI domain will be co-decided by Apple and Google, as this chapter will show. Given the edge that the two companies have in AI and data, they will become important market leaders in the lucrative healthcare sector, where many recent breakthroughs rely on data and AI.

Chapter 4 surveys existing global legal protections that might restrict the power of app stores. It starts by focusing on the US. In the US, the Federal Trade Commission enacted some of the first explicit rules for app stores in 2013. However, because this agency has traditionally preferred industry self-regulation over explicit lawmaking, these rules have only been partially implemented and have not been reviewed since. In addition, the EU has long tried to regulate software using a principle based, technology neutral approach. The GDPR is the most well-known example of this. However, by not being more explicit and technology specific, the EU has ended up having the strong principles that are behind its regulation poorly followed in app ecosystems. Because the self-regulatory and principle based approaches struggle in digital platforms, lawmakers are increasingly adopting explicit platform regulation, particularly the DSA and DMA in the EU. These laws acknowledge the fundamental role that some online platforms play and establish a wide array of obligations to protect individuals from systemic risks that arise from these platforms, given that these laws are new and need to be further interpreted by the courts. Therefore, the most immediate change to the established ways of working in app ecosystems might arise from the wealth of ongoing actions in court based on long-standing laws. These try to enforce other non-technology specific bodies of law within app ecosystems, such as competition and consumer protection laws. However, this approach brings many challenges, as will be discussed in detail. In conclusion, the providers of app stores continue to face limited explicit legal obligations and have mainly been considered in a footnote, similar to most previous academic studies on online platforms. The contribution of this chapter lies in the fact that it is the first coherent and current account that details the legal obligations that the providers of app stores face in the EU and the US.

Readers who are familiar with EU and US law regarding app stores might want to proceed to the next chapter. The same might be true for readers who are not overly interested in the underlying legal issues. A deep understanding of the applicable laws is not required to understand the other chapters.

Chapter 5 gives an overview of the relevant methodologies for app analysis and of important previous work on studying app stores. The educational material in this chapter has been developed in collaboration with leading UK digital rights organisations. Therefore, it promises to be particularly helpful for those individuals and organisations new to the study of app stores who wish to attain the necessary technical skills for data collection and analysis. This chapter discusses the two primary methods for the study of mobile apps: (1) dynamic; and (2) static app analysis. In brief, dynamic analysis reveals apps' workings by running them on an actual device, and static analysis tries to analyse apps without ever running them. With the rise of natural language processing and the release of Apple and Google's Privacy Nutrition Labels, a new approach to app analysis has emerged: privacy policy and label analysis. These new methods are also covered. This chapter discusses how intentional decisions by Apple and Google have had negative effects on researchers seeking to study app privacy and, therefore, negative effects on data protection and privacy more generally. In addition, this chapter tests and documents how data could be accessed from the app stores using the DSA but finds that its practical relevance remains limited and that it'll take longer until the law becomes more helpful, or not.

Chapters 6–9 explore a variety of (systemic) risks that emerge from actions by Apple and Google in their respective app ecosystems. The contribution of these chapters lies in the fact that they detail how (technical) decisions by Apple and Google concern economic and market considerations and have an effect on a wide range of fundamental rights and freedoms.

Chapter 6 explores app monetisation and content moderation on the app stores, including Apple's dependence on China. Notable content moderation decisions by Apple and Google, such as banning apps like Parler or Disconnect.me, are discussed. These decisions often appear inconsistent or politically motivated, raising concerns about arbitrary enforcement. Meanwhile, disputes over monetisation policies, such as Apple's 30 per cent App Store commission, highlight the restrictive environment developers face. In conclusion, this chapter underlines that action against Apple and Google's market power has, in the past, focused a lot on market outcomes and not much on the broader systemic risks posed by the actions of these companies.

Chapter 7 studies the concepts of data protection and privacy, and underlines problems with the rule of law on the app stores. These concepts have come to the forefront of societal discussions via notable data breaches, such as Cambridge Analytica, and Apple's widely circulated market claim that 'Privacy. That's iPhone.' Because none of the chapters assume prior legal knowledge, this chapter first introduces the reader to what privacy means and points out that it is highly individual. Therefore, data protection and privacy laws tend to focus on the protection of data relating to individuals (personal data), and data protection has emerged as a separate right, in addition to the right to privacy, in the EU, UK, and other jurisdictions. Then, this chapter delves into contemporary problems around privacy in apps, zooms in on the concept of real time bidding (a particularly invasive form of mobile advertising), outlines the example of the Grindr app and how it shared the HIV status of its LGBTQ users with advertisers for profit, and shed lights on the debate of whether users could ever have a choice over how data is processed (as claimed by Apple and many other advertising companies). Then, this chapter becomes more technical. It considers the evolution of privacy (protections) in mobile apps and how the app store infrastructure facilitates large-scale data collection (also known as 'tracking'). In conclusion, while legal initiatives such as the GDPR aimed to bolster data protection and privacy, they have not managed to make fundamental changes to the data economy and change the strong underlying economic incentives.

Chapter 8 zooms in on health and autonomy. It discusses how the adoption of smartphones has coincided with an immense increase in mental health problems, particularly in young children. The design of apps and the app economy might have played a role in these outcomes, especially when apps integrate addictive design patterns, as they widely do. This chapter explores Apple and Google's design philosophies behind their app ecosystems, discusses the measures they have taken to restrict personal autonomy in their respective platforms, and illustrates what has been driving this change. To this end, this chapter draws on a historical perspective and traces the evolution of software from desktop (which traditionally used to allow much more customisation) to mobile. As a specific example, the design concepts of skeuomorphism (which models software design on real world artefacts) and minimalism are discussed, as well as how recent iterations of mobile operating systems have shifted to the latter. It highlights that these shifts in thinking and design are not confined to mobile ecosystems but are part of broader, worldwide trends towards increased simplicity and a loss of individuality. Given that so many hours are spent looking at our phones, our expectations from the real world should be significantly shaped by the designs that are observed in apps and that are partly controlled by the design guidelines and app components of Apple and Google.

Chapter 9 looks beyond smartphones and tablets and shows how many of the paradigms underpinning the two have created new forms of technology, particularly the Internet of Things (IoT), and affected existing ones. As part of this, this chapter looks into how modern cars, being powered by electric motors and batteries, increasingly become 'smartphones with wheels' and how personal computers and modern mobile technology have mutually reinforced innovations in each other. In addition, it looks into e-readers, smartwatches, smart TVs, and lethal drones in Russia's war against Ukraine, all of which run (partly) on smartphone technology, for example, derivatives of Android and iOS. This chapter finds that the advent of smartphone technology has brought along a new paradigm for software development that has spread across many industries. This paradigm tends to allow the faster development of IT products because hardware and software components are widely reused. However, it could negatively impact environmental protection and sustainability. For example, smartphone derived products, including cars, widely use lithium ion batteries, which are often difficult to replace and recycle. In addition, they degrade over time. Another example is that the lifetime of these IT products widely depends on support from the manufacturer. Products often come to a premature end when the manufacturer no longer supplies software updates. All this, at least in the smartphone industry, creates an average lifespan of 2.5 years, after which the products are usually discarded. The actions of Apple and Google play a role in these outcomes. Moving forward, this book highlights that smartphone technology is commonly used in modern warfare, and that tech companies, not just Apple and Google, are probably going to get involved more in the lucrative defence sector in the future.

Finally, this book turns its look ahead to the future and towards the conclusions, in three parts.

Chapter 10 introduces a framework to discuss the power that Apple and Google exert over society. It is argued that there are three important elements to that power: (1) core values; (2) behaviours; and (3) risks and outcomes from that behaviour. These core values are identified as Anglo-libertarian morals, shareholder value, and technological edge, intertwined with tech solutionism. They lead to a range of behaviour, which in turn leads to various (systemic) risks and outcomes, as discussed throughout this book.

Chapter 11 reflects on how the (systemic) risks identified throughout the book could be responded to. After all, Apple and Google must take reasonable actions against systemic risks under the DSA. Therefore, this book makes a range of suggestions, including a more explicit duty of care, the establishment of democratic elements for app platform governance, a right to repair for end users, a new approach to technology regulation that is agile and technology specific (in stark contrast to previous principle based and technology neutral regulatory approaches for the digital economy), the need to strengthen platform data access, the divestment of app infrastructure into independent organisations, and the need to increase the sustainability and security of the app economy.

Chapter 12 provides concluding thoughts.

PART I

Foundations

2

An Introduction to the App
Economy for Non-Techies

Before going into any details, it is worthwhile to introduce the foundations behind the app economy and explain what apps are and consist of, how developers make them, and how they are distributed to end users.

2.1 What is an app?

App packages (apps) are the foundational parts of the app economy. At their core, these are mere '.zip' archives, similar to those we download all the time from the internet. The difference between apps and arbitrary '.zip' files from the internet is that app packages follow a specific format. App packages contain: (1) the app binary; (2) further app resources; (3) descriptive metadata; and (4) a signature. The focus on a single file makes apps different from traditional software for desktops, which is often spread across multiple files. It makes these apps significantly more straightforward to distribute and update, especially when using a centralised app store.

The core of an app package is the app binary. This file contains the instructions that the smartphone follows when a user opens the app. These instructions include, among other aspects, how to react to user inputs, what to display to the user, how to use phone sensors, such as the Global Positioning System (GPS) and gyroscope, how to store user data, and how to retrieve additional data from the internet. On iOS, the instructions in the app binary are 'arm64' instructions, which can be directly understood by the iPhone central processing unit (CPU). The CPU is the 'brain' of any computer, including smartphones, that carries out all the necessary computations to respond to user interactions and show content on the device screen.

Meanwhile, on Android, the instructions are usually in the form of bytecode. Unlike arm64 instructions, bytecode cannot be directly understood by Android CPUs. Instead, it must first be translated into instructions suitable for each specific smartphone upon app installation. This reflects the openness of the Android ecosystem to various manufacturers, as opposed to the tight vertical integration of iOS.

While an app could run with just the binary, most apps rely on additional app resources included in the app package. These resources may include sounds, images, video, user interface (UI) layout files, configuration files, and third-party libraries. Storing these files separately from the app binary has several advantages, including faster app startup times. On Android, '.xml' layout files play an important role because they describe how the app is shown to the user at run-time.

Additional metadata is stored in an 'Info.plist' file on iOS and an 'AndroidManifest.xml' file on Android. Both files contain, among other aspects, information about the app title, the compatibility of the app with various iOS or Android versions, and the permissions, such as calendar or camera access, that the app can request. Additionally, the metadata contains an app identifier that serves as a global permanent identifier of an app across the local smartphone and app store. Because the app identifier is global and permanent, it cannot be changed after the release of an app on an app store. Even if an app is withdrawn from one of the app stores, another app developer can never reuse the same app identifier.

The signature, now standard on iOS and Android, ensures the app's integrity and verifies the authenticity of the app developer behind the app. This ensures that attackers cannot easily trick users into installing malicious apps, such as those that claim to be developed by Meta or Facebook but are not.

2.2 How is an app made?

Apps are usually made using one of two tools: (1) Android Studio for Android; and (2) Xcode for iOS. These tools, called integrated development environments (IDEs), can be downloaded for free from Google's, resp. (Apple's, official) website. Nowadays (unlike in the early days of smartphones), they make the development of apps relatively straightforward. All that is required is knowledge of the relevant programming language. The remaining knowledge can be obtained from the online documentation provided by Google and Apple, online forums like Stack Overflow, and increasingly large-language models (LLMs), such as ChatGPT and GitHub Copilot. Of course, learning how to program apps still takes a lot of time.

Android Studio is compatible with Windows, macOS, and Linux, and Xcode, sadly, only runs on Apple's macOS.

Until recently, Java was the only programming language for Android and Objective-C for iOS. Google chose Java when it launched Android because it has long been one of the most widely used programming languages. This made it relatively easy for app developers to start coding for Android.

Meanwhile, Apple chose Objective-C because it had long been the primary programming language that software developers used to develop its macOS desktop operating system. Nowadays, developers can, alternatively, choose Kotlin for Android and Swift for iOS; both are relatively new programming languages; however, they tend to be easier to write and also prevent mistakes when programming.

The IDEs, Android Studio and Xcode, contain a wide array of tools that try to make the development of mobile apps as easy as possible. In theory, all that would be needed to develop an app for either Android or iOS would be a text editor; this would be relatively cumbersome. Key features of IDEs are automatic code completion and verification, a visual designer for app user interfaces, and a device emulator. Automatic code competition and verification significantly reduce development time and programming errors. The visual designer makes it easy to design app interfaces as developers wish. Interface elements, such as buttons or text fields, can simply be dragged into the app and moved around. The device emulator allows software developers to run their own apps directly inside a window on their computer. This enables developers to test apps quickly on a variety of different devices, even if they don't own a physical device. However, physical devices can and should be used during app development because they might still behave differently compared with the emulation.

The development process for mobile apps is often highly iterative. A developer makes small changes to the app code or design and then tests these changes on the device emulator or physical device. This iterative process is facilitated by the app store model, which makes the rollout of even the smallest changes quick, simple, and seamless. This is why many apps on your phone are updated almost every week or even more frequently.

The IDEs also allow the easy integration of third-party libraries. These libraries contain lines of code developed by other companies, for example, to monetise or evaluate user interactions. The most popular third-party libraries are Google Ads and Google Analytics, both developed and maintained by Google. The advantage of third-party libraries is that they save app developers valuable programming time by allowing them to reuse code developed by other companies. It also helps reduce any errors in programming, especially if the code behind the library is used by thousands of different apps or is available open source and, therefore, for anyone to verify.

However, by using third-party libraries, the app developer also gives up a certain degree of agency over the software development process. This is because the code of libraries is usually integrated directly into the app, potentially giving third-party companies access to the same user data as the app. Many libraries, including Google Ads and Google Analytics, are closed source computer code. This means that a developer who wants to use these libraries can never see the underlying code and what instructions will be run inside their app by those libraries. Despite these security concerns, there is essentially no app that doesn't use any such libraries. Ample previous research has underlined that the use of such third-party libraries by developers makes them dependent on privacy invasive data practices that involve the processing of large amounts of personal data (Greene and Shilton, 2018; Ó Fathaigh et al, 2018; Mhaidli et al, 2019), with little awareness from users and app developers (Solove, 2012; Reyes et al, 2018; Datenschutzkonferenz, 2019; Zimmeck et al, 2019).

The relationship between some of the main actors in the app economy is shown in Figure 2.1.

The fact that Android and iOS use different programming environments and languages creates significant costs for companies wishing to develop mobile apps. In most countries, Android and iOS are used by a considerable share of individuals, and any company that wants to reach the largest number of individuals must develop for both platforms. Some alternatives to Android Studio and Xcode exist that allow developers to write one code base for both iOS and Android; they usually lag behind the official tooling in terms of ease of use, speed of the app, and natural look of the resulting app. As a result, specialised firms are often necessary to develop apps. This is why one usually distinguishes between the app developer and app publisher, with the latter being the company that ultimately puts the developed app on the

Figure 2.1: The main actors in the ad-financed mobile app economy

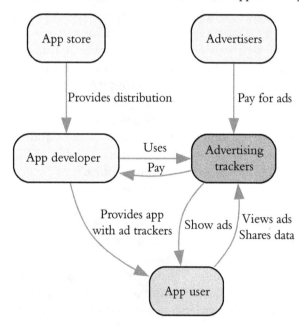

market. This book, for simplicity, does not make this distinction and just refers to 'app developers.'

Finally, the IDEs allow the code to be turned into an app package to be uploaded to the relevant app stores.

2.3 What is an app store?

The app stores on Android (Google Play Store) and iOS (Apple App Store) serve as the central entry point to the available apps for each platform. Besides Apple and Google, app stores have two main stakeholders: app users and developers.

Through app stores, users can easily explore new apps, find apps they already know, and install them on their smartphones. This presents a significant convenience for users compared with desktop software. On desktop computers, traditionally, there hasn't been a similar centralised resource for software distribution. Instead, users usually had to access the website of the company behind a piece of software, download (and potentially purchase) it from there, and then manually install the software. The installation process is usually somewhat different for each desktop program. A similar observation can be made for the update process for desktop programs, which is often cumbersome. Meanwhile, on app stores, installation is usually just a click away, and updating happens automatically in the background without any further user interaction.

Maybe the most important, and also most controversial aspect, is the fact that app stores can play an essential role in building user trust in the quality and security of software. For example, desktop computers have been plagued by malware for many years. Malware has long been less common on app stores, although mobile apps have repeatedly been distributed widely and turned out to be malware. Ensuring the security of millions of apps, many of which are updated regularly, is a colossal task. Therefore, reviewing every line of code of every app is infeasible and must rely on heuristics, which inherently have vulnerabilities and gaps. This is also why the UK Competition and Markets Authority (CMA) found that the security benefits of mobile apps, compared with desktops, are often somewhat exaggerated (Competition and Markets Authority, 2022b).

Users could download and install apps from outside the Play Store on Android, but not on iOS. Here, the App Store had long been the only resource. Apple simply did not permit any alternative app stores. Interestingly, Google has also implemented various strategies to restrict the distribution of alternative app stores, such as a ban on distributing such stores on the Play Store. With the DMA from 2022, this is now changing, as will be discussed in Section 4.3. Whether this will change the status quo regarding the dominance of Apple and Google in the app economy remains doubtful.

App stores come with relatively natural effects of scale because many users appreciate the simplicity of having a single central point for app distribution.

Once app developers have turned their app code into an app package with the relevant IDE (see the previous section), they can upload this package to the app store and make it available to users. Google and Apple review all submissions to their app stores and verify compliance with their app store policies. These policies, among other aspects, contain details on what types of data apps are allowed to access (for example, apps solely aimed at children aren't allowed to use location on Android) and what apps look like. A standard critique of the app review process is that it can be opaque and inconsistent. Neither Apple nor Google, to prevent companies from trying to game the app review process, publishes the exact steps that are followed during the app review. This lack of transparency and accountability reinforces the power imbalance between the app store operators and the app developers, who are entirely dependent on the sometimes arbitrary app review decisions (Greene and Shilton, 2018). This issue is the subject of ongoing investigation by authorities who are concerned that Apple and Google may abuse their market power (Competition and Markets Authority, 2022b) and sometimes insufficiently review apps, thereby causing potential harm to end-users (for example, under the DSA). These elements will be discussed more in Chapter 4.

App stores even handle all in-app purchases of digital goods, including subscriptions, on behalf of the app developers. This arguably allows app developers to spend more time on software development. This also means that app developers give up significant control, including paying the app stores hefty commissions of up to 30 per cent on any transactions. As such, this might also considerably harm consumers who ultimately have to pay these commissions and are thus subject to ongoing investigations by courts and authorities. This will be discussed further in Section 4.4.

As part of the app stores, Apple (App Analytics) and Google (Play Console) collect detailed download statistics and make these accessible to developers, providing basic analytics to developers even without integrating analytics tracking libraries. This underlines the critical role that app stores play, both in making apps available to end users and providing app developers with the relevant data to build sustainable digital businesses.

2.4 What is a mobile operating system?

The mobile app ecosystem has two leading mobile operating systems (OS): Android and iOS. They provide the foundation upon which apps and app stores run. They are like Dr House and Wilson. Without House, there'd be no Wilson. Without Wilson, there'd be no House.

The mobile OS manages the phone's resources, including the CPU for computing tasks, phone storage, battery, network antennae, camera, and other peripherals. Nowadays, they are some of the most intricate and sophisticated pieces of software, being the foundation for the day-to-day interactions between millions of people around the globe.

In managing the CPU and battery, the OS ensures that all apps have a fair share of the resources to complete their tasks. For example, when the battery runs low, the operating system may decide to prioritise the app running in the foreground and delay downloading the latest emails in the background.

The OS also plays a pivotal role in phone security. Being the gatekeeper to all the phone's functionalities, the OS ensures that apps run safely and in isolation and cannot access the resources of the phone or other apps without adequate permission. This includes the separation of data between apps, which is different from how data has traditionally been handled on desktop computers. Here, traditionally, programs tended to have access to other programs' data, which can present a security and privacy risk. It also includes various privacy features, as discussed in Section 7.3.

One of the key differences between iOS and Android is the fact that the latter is available in an open source fashion. While Google takes the lead in the development of Android, independent developers have access to the program code behind it and can develop and distribute their own versions. However, this comes with an important catch: many apps will not work correctly without additional, closed source components on an Android phone. This principally includes the Google Play Services. These bring notification, authentication, online data storage, and many other functionalities to Android phones. Without them, logging in to many apps, receiving notifications, and many other things become impossible. Installing the Google Play Services is mandatory for all phone manufacturers that wish to include the Google Play Store. Given that this is the only major Android app store (outside of China), phone manufacturers do not have a choice.

The operating systems also play an essential role in collecting data about end users. On Android, the Google Play Services facilitate data collection as part of Google Ads, Google Analytics, and Google Firebase Analytics (microg, no date), with currently no options for end users to turn off this data processing. This implies that every Android phone with access to the Google Play Store comes with extensive user tracking functionality. This raises concerns about whether end users are fully informed and have consented to this practice when making their purchase decision (Gamba et al, 2020). The French data protection regulator – the Commission Nationale de l'Informatique et des Libertés (CNIL) – found this was not the case and fined Google over its design of the Android ecosystem and the lack of transparency in 2019 (Commission Nationale de l'Informatique et des Libertés, 2019). Google subsequently changed the design of its consent screens.

On iOS, the system library SKAdNetwork facilitates the attribution of clicks on ads (see Section 7.3.4) without using user identifiers, thereby reducing the ability of trackers to build profiles about users. However, this 'privacy preserving' approach by Apple also discloses information about users' ad clicks to Apple, which could use this data to build user profiles for its own advertising business. Indeed, the company claims in its privacy policy that it might use users' 'interactions with ads delivered by Apple's advertising platform' (Apple, 2024b), which includes third party advertisements that use the SKAdNetwork. Upon request using my GDPR rights, Apple confirmed this to me, after an illegal 6-month delay and two complaints to data protection authorities. Over its ad tracking on iOS without consent, Apple was fined €8 million by the French data protection authority CNIL in late 2022 (Commission Nationale de l'Informatique et des Libertés, 2023). Other cases against Apple's changes are ongoing.

Overall, Android – resp. iOS – operating systems share data with Google – resp. Apple – at high frequency, in great detail, and with limited user choice (Leith, 2021; Kollnig et al, 2022b). These findings conflict with Apple's marketing promises that iOS would be a more privacy preserving ecosystem, as will be discussed in more detail in Chapter 7.

2.5 A drastic change in how to make IT

The centralised model of mobile apps, focusing on self-contained app packages distributed through a centralised app store and tailor-made for the underlying mobile OS, comes with many advantages. These include a high degree of convenience for end users when using apps and a streamlined environment for developers to create and distribute apps. The centralisation of control also comes with downsides. As it stands, Apple and Google, in their respective ecosystem, possess a high degree of control across the supply chain, including third-party libraries, IDEs, operating systems, user monitoring and data collection, and app stores. This opens up these app ecosystems to an abuse of platform power, as will be explored in the following chapters.

3

A Brief History of the App Economy: From Landline to AI

The app economy constitutes a radical departure from previous computing paradigms, which started with the release of the iPhone in 2007 and the Apple App Store in 2008. The history of the app economy is visualised in Figure 3.1 and summarised in the following, to set the scene for the later chapters.

3.1 Before the iPhone

In some regards, 'non-smart' mobile phones could be seen as a predecessor to smartphones. After all, smartphones have the same telecommunication functionality as phones. It is possible to send and receive SMS and make phone calls. However, today's smartphones' ease of use and breadth of functionality go well beyond those of the infamous Nokia 3310 and its relatives. All this was made possible by putting desktop-grade computing chips into portable devices. As such, smartphones are instead the next logical step from portable computers, which descended from regular desktop computers.

The iPhone was not the first smartphone to make advanced computing facilities available on the go. The Canadian company Blackberry is often credited with inventing the modern smartphone, bringing internet-enabled services, including email, onto mobile phones. However, the Blackberry lacked a crucial feature that allowed the iPhone to be extensible in myriad ways and led to the emergence of millions of apps: the touch screen. BlackBerry eventually failed because of this.

The promise of a touch screen was simple: rather than have physical buttons (like the Blackberry that featured a full QWERTY keyboard), the touch input makes it more flexible in terms of how users interact with software. Rather than having to match the app with whatever buttons were available on the phone, a touchscreen allows the inputs to match what an app

Figure 3.1: Overview of some of the key developments in the app economy over the past two decades

Pre-2007
PDAs, Blackberry devices, and
early touchscreen devices (e.g. Nintendo DS)

2007
Launch of the first Apple iPhone

2008
Launch of the Apple App Store and Android Market

2009
Launch of WhatsApp

2011
SMS messaging peaks with 2.4 trillion messages sent

2017
International launch of TikTok

2018
GDPR comes into effect in Europe

2021
Google acquires Fitbit

2022
Launch of ChatGPT

requires. Touch input with our fingers is also arguably much more natural than pressing mechanical buttons.

Again, the iPhone wasn't the first mobile phone to feature a touchscreen. Many attempts have been made to use touch features in 21st-century computing. The most prominent example is the Nintendo DS, which allows users to interact with a stylus, a special pen for interactions with the touchscreen. Similarly, personal digital assistants (PDAs) used to be smartphones that allowed user input with a stylus. They often, additionally, featured a full-fledged keyboard because the input of text with a stylus tended to be cumbersome.

Why, then, did engineers at the time not simply forget about the stylus and allow people to use their own hands for user input? This is because the touchscreens used in devices before the iPhone were single-touch screens. Multiple touches would confuse these screens. Precise input was required, which could only be delivered with a stylus. This wasn't a great user experience.

The iPhone was different. It was the first device to use and make multi touch screens broadly available, which made it possible to use multiple fingers at a time and overcome the reliance on the stylus. In addition, smartphones provide rich sensory information (such as a GPS, gyroscope, accelerometer, and camera), which has further contributed to the kind of apps that can be built for this platform.

3.2 Towards mass adoption, changing industries

From the release of the iPhone, it took quite a few years until smartphones reached mass adoption. At the same time, they happened to be one of the fastest adopted new technologies to date. It took slightly over 5 years to reach more than 50 per cent of the US market. In comparison, it took personal computers, television screens, or electricity decades to achieve a similar feat. This is a testament to the immense versatility of the technology and relative affordability. These days, while many people in developing countries may not possess a regular computer, smartphones have become ubiquitous even in the most remote corners of the planet.

As smartphones have become widely adopted, they have turned many previously existing industries upside down. One of the most obvious ones might be communication.

3.2.1 Communication

When Apple launched the first iPhone in June 2007, the communication landscape was quite different from today. MySpace was the most popular social media platform at that time. Facebook was just emerging and struggling immensely with adapting
to mobile apps. The most common messaging apps outside of China were Windows Live Messenger, Skype, Yahoo, AIM, and ICQ. Apart from Facebook (now Meta), none remained market leaders. Instead, new services have emerged.

WhatsApp was among the first and most famous of these new communication services. It was only launched in November 2009. Within 2 years, WhatsApp replaced SMS as the dominant model for text messages. SMS peaked in 2011 at 2.4 trillion messages sent (Statista, 2022c). The makers of WhatsApp realised that they could provide a more attractive messaging service than SMS (and MMS, its multimedia counterpart) by sending messages over the data connection in smartphones. Rather than paying for each message or expensive messaging plans, users traditionally only had to pay an annual $1 charge for WhatsApp.

Soon after the release of WhatsApp, two new social media and messaging apps emerged: Instagram in 2010 and Snapchat in 2011. Both apps allow users to share photos with friends and others. Initially, Snapchat emphasised the direct sharing of self-destructing photos between individual users (such as sexual images); Instagram focused on building a social media platform around photos. The rise of these apps was tightly linked to the increased capabilities of smartphones. The 3G standard was launched in 2002; however, it was not fast enough to support data-heavy smartphone apps. Neither the upload nor the download speeds were fast enough. Instead, only the 3.5G (also known as HSPA) and 4G (also known as LTE) standards, which were started to be deployed in the late 2000s, could meet the requirements. TikTok was launched much later: in China in 2016 and internationally in 2017. At the time, we were slowly moving into the 5G era. These developments underline how closely innovation in hardware affects software and, thereby, how we function as a society.

The rise of new forms of social interactions also brought new forms of monetisation and information sharing. News editors had traditionally curated news, but algorithmically produced social media feeds now increasingly take up this role. The influence of algorithms on public opinion, for example, in shaping the outcomes of elections, remains hotly debated, not least since Cambridge Analytica. The influence of social media on public elections is sometimes exaggerated, especially since other media outlets, such as television, still have significant shares among individuals and are often the primary channels for these individuals to retrieve political information. However, this is likely to change as more individuals who have grown up with smartphones and do not consume any other media besides mobile-based information engage in elections. We have already seen this in the 2024 elections in Bulgaria, Romania, and Moldova, where it has been argued that the Russian state very successfully interfered, including through sophisticated social media campaigns.

What can be said, though, is that modern social media has democratised, for better and worse, who shapes public opinion. The influence of a university educated elite, who used to dominate news publishing, has declined, while non-traditional voices find it easier to reach audiences. This has, for example, been demonstrated during Trump's presidency. He violated many of the traditional norms in media and engaged directly with its voters (and haters) through Twitter on his phone. His Twitter use frequently peaked during Fox & Friends, a daily news show he often commented on. Famously, on 2 January 2018, he tweeted that his 'Nuclear Button' was 'much bigger & more powerful' than Kim Jong-Un's, only minutes after a segment on Kim's nuclear button.

The rise of social media undermined the traditional model of funding news and led to the decline of countless news outlets, especially local ones. At the same time, it is well-known that independent quality journalism is essential to reduce the inefficiency of public finances and fight corruption (Gao et al, 2020).

The societal influence of smartphones is vast and growing. Apple and Google play an essential role in how this plays out. Chapter 6 will discuss their content moderation and the effects of this in more detail.

3.2.2 Gaming

Besides communication, gaming is one of the app economy's most critical and transformative elements. Indeed, it is the most lucrative element of the app economy, at least when only looking at direct spending on app stores (that is, excluding advertising on social media and online search). Revenues from games accounted for two-thirds of what was generated via apps in 2022 (Statista, 2023d).

As social media has done to communication and news, mobile gaming has managed to democratise the gaming industry in many ways. Expensive hardware, such as PCs or consoles, is no longer necessary. Gaming has become more casual and accessible. Whenever someone is on a long bus or train ride, this presents an opportunity to engage in gaming that did not exist before smartphones. This has created a massive market. In 2021, the video gaming industry made a total revenue of about $180 billion, approximately 50 per cent coming from mobile gaming, 30 per cent from consoles, and 20 per cent from PC games (VentureBeat, 2021). By adopting smartphones, we've come a long way in overcoming boredom and commodifying our day-to-day interactions. This commodification, apparently, even extends to bathroom visits of two-thirds of smartphone users ...

Of course, mobile handhelds, such as the PlayStation Portable or the Nintendo DS, had been around longer than smartphones. However, while the DS was the best-selling handheld ever made, it 'only' sold about 150 million units worldwide. This is in stark contrast to the 3 billion mobile gamers that exist nowadays, a factor of 20 more (Statista, 2021b), and underlines the extreme speed at which smartphones have revolutionised society. Therefore, Chapter 11 will develop some ideas on how to keep up with this speed in law and regulation.

This ubiquity of smartphones has reduced the entry threshold and thereby changed gamers' profiles. About 20 years ago, over 70 per cent of gamers were male, and females were just a small minority (In An Age, 2014). Nowadays, about half of mobile gamers are female (Statista, 2021a). One reason for the increase in female players is the broader set of available games. Casual games (for example, puzzles, word, and card games) are particularly widely used by female players (Statista, 2021a).

Besides the mere adoption of smartphones, another driver for the spread of gaming has been the change in business models. High upfront investment on console hardware and games used to be necessary (which often ran into hundreds of dollars), but the most successful games nowadays are available at zero price. Therefore, companies can cater to a global audience of gamers with diverse ability levels to pay.

Zero price does, of course, not mean that most apps are now free. Companies still need to fund their operations and pay their programmers to assemble all the apps. Most zero price games use a combination of in-app purchases, subscriptions, and advertising to monetise. Chapter 6 will discuss monetisation more; however, all three of these approaches rely on collecting vast amounts of user data so that monetisation can be improved and fine-tuned. This can adversely affect privacy, as discussed in Chapter 7. All types of monetisation tend to imply that more time spent translates into more revenue, for example, because more adverts can be shown. Many of the most popular games have been found using design patterns that increase usage time, make gamers 'hooked', and cause users to lose control of spending (Eyal and Hoover, 2013). This will be discussed more in Chapter 8.

One example of these engagement increasing design patterns is in-game currencies that can be bought for real money. This 'virtual' money then allows purchasing in-game items and encourages losing track of spending. Another design pattern is the so-called 'loot boxes' that can be purchased by users and contain a set of random items, some of which bring tangible benefits to the gamer. While there are almost always some returns, they are usually relatively meagre or undesirable. This makes loot boxes similar to slot machines in casinos, whose addictive potential has been proven. Children, who tend to have much more limited self-control than adults, and those with a history of addiction are most susceptible to these design patterns. As a result, loot boxes have been classified as 'gambling' and restricted in an increasing number of countries, for example, in China (Xiao, 2020), Belgium (Xiao, 2023), and Austria (GamesIndustry, 2023), although with mixed success (Xiao, 2023). Chapter 8 will discuss the health implications of smartphones in more detail.

Interestingly, it has been reported that 0.15 per cent of gamers account for 50 per cent of the revenues generated from games (Takahashi, 2014). This highlights that 'hardcore' players drive the returns from mobile gaming and that the financial effects of mobile gaming are very unevenly distributed. When designing monetisation, app developers need to walk a thin line between giving benefits to paying users and not unfairly disadvantaging non-paying users who might otherwise quit the game for a competitor. Some apps additionally offer a 'paid' version, which usually comes with more features and fewer ads.

The education and learning community has also picked up the spread of mobile gaming and sophisticated design schemes to keep end users hooked. They are trying to gamify the education experience, aiming to make learning more attractive (and create a fantastic business out of it). Duolingo is one of the most well-known examples of these apps, which has turned language learning into a successful game. The app's philosophy is that spending a few minutes every day is enough to reach a working proficiency once the lessons for a given language are finished. This can sometimes take several years, and a lot more effort on the part of learners. It is also not free because users must see adverts or pay for a premium subscription. As such, Duolingo is incentivised to keep learners hooked but not necessarily to help them finish learning a language. This is especially true as Duolingo is a publicly traded company with annual revenues of about $400 million in 2023 (Statista, 2023c). In any case, Duolingo employs a range of noteworthy strategies to keep learners motivated. These include tracking of learning streaks (for example, consecutive days of learning), experience points and badges for achievements, leader boards and competition with other players, an immersive audio-visual experience, and creative notifications and reminders (for example, 'Hi, it's Duo. Just waiting to learn some French with you [smiling emoji]'). The company claims that, in the US, more people are learning foreign languages via Duolingo than in the public school system.

3.2.3 Health

In the coming years, one of the biggest sectors for the app economy will be the health sector. After all, populations across the globe are getting older, and more digitally savvy at the same time. Apple and Google will take a leading role, and once again, use their market power in existing industries to become dominant in others. The two companies taking the lead on digital contract tracing, as described in the Introduction, were among the first very notable signs of this trend.

The health sector tends to be extremely lucrative for the big players and constitutes a major part of many economies. In high-income countries, expenditure on health care typically is around 10 per cent of the GDP; in the US, this figure stands at 17 per cent (World Health Organization, 2023). As such, health care dwarfs the annual revenues of the major tech companies, as shown in Figure 3.2. This also creates a massive business opportunity for

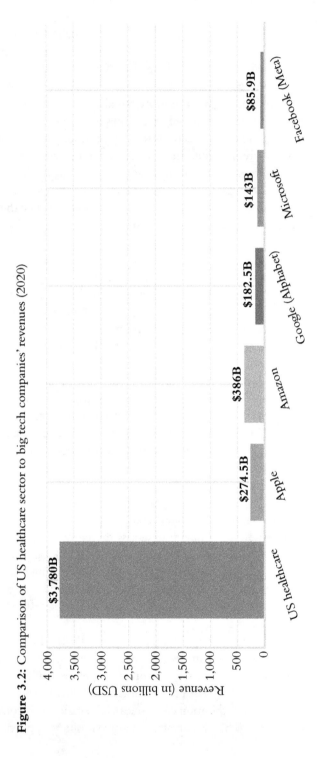

Figure 3.2: Comparison of US healthcare sector to big tech companies' revenues (2020)

them, given that they are leading the IT sector and that many breakthroughs in medicine are driven by artificial intelligence (AI) technologies.

We can already see how the big tech companies are driving innovation in the health sector. AlphaFold, released by Google's subsidiary DeepMind in 2018, solved a key problem in modern-day biology: protein folding. For these successes, two Google DeepMind researchers won the 2024 Nobel Prize in Chemistry (because there is no Nobel Prize for medicine).

Looking back, one of the first successful fitness apps was Runkeeper, released for Android and iOS shortly after the App Store and Android Market were launched in 2008. The app allows individuals to use the GPS sensor on their smartphone to track their outdoor runs, including pace, distance, and time. Fitbit, founded in 2007, launched its first Fitbit device in 2009, taking the concept of Runkeeper a step further. Rather than just tracking the GPS location, its devices enabled users to track various parameters related to their health, including step count, heart rate, blood oxygen, and menstrual cycle. It has become a one-stop shop for everything health-related and a pioneer in the market for 'wearables'. Its main competitor, the Apple Watch, was only launched in 2015. The Apple Watch turned out to be a massive success; however, Google never managed to develop its own competing product. It ended up acquiring Fitbit for $ 2.1 billion in 2021. Chapter 9 will look further into these portable devices and some of the challenges they bring, including for sustainability and warfare.

Another hugely successful app in the space is the Headspace app, which was launched in 2010. Rather than enabling users to track their sports activities, this app tries to provide users with meditation and relaxation exercises wherever they are, and thereby neatly makes use of smartphones' unique characteristics. In 2021, the company was valued at $3 billion (TechCrunch, 2021b). Besides, Google and Apple operate so-called 'health' apps that serve as a central location for data storage and syncing across an individual's various apps and tools for their health and fitness. As a result, the two companies increasingly hold more detailed data about the health and fitness of individuals than any other healthcare provider, putting them in a privileged position in the digital economy where data tends to be everything.

The increased use of smartphones for sensitive health data is not without concerns and has been subject to intense scrutiny. For example, the Norwegian data protection authority revealed in May 2016 that Runkeeper was continuously sharing location data with advertisers (even when not running) and did so without adequately disclosing these practices in its privacy policy (Android Authority, 2016). In the case of Fitbit's acquisition, Google had to promise to the European Commission not to use 'health and wellness data collected from wrist-worn wearable devices' for advertising, among other remedies (European Commission, 2020).

Moving forward, as Apple and Google are under pressure to diversify their revenues and keep growing, we will likely see further activities on their part to snap up a part of countries' large healthcare budgets.

3.3 Wearables and AI (assistants)

The app economy has, in the past, vastly changed how computing works. But it is unlikely that this is the end of the story. Instead, the app economy has routinely spilled into other industries and further developed with technological progress.

One strand of significant technological advances has been the size of computing devices. Smartphones managed to advance the boundaries when it comes to high computing facilities in a tiny space. For example, this led to the birth of the Internet of Things (IoT) and wearables. One of the most well-known examples is the Apple Watch smartwatch, which allows easy access to one's apps and tracking one's day-to-day activities. While many individuals love this, there is also a strong industry behind this. By pushing computing into more and more aspects of our lives, they also gain more control over them. In the healthcare sector, COVID-19 apps (as discussed in the Introduction) and smartwatches are illustrative examples of this (Sharon, 2020). More of this technical evolution will be discussed in Chapter 9.

The underlying behaviour of large tech companies was termed 'sphere transgressions' (Sharon, 2023). She observed that, again and again, tech companies gain dominance in one sector of our lives and then use this to conquer another sector. Being a philosopher, she worries about the ethics and legitimacy of this. After all, tech companies usually do not have much prior expertise in these new sectors. Their legitimacy solely arises from their technical dominance and ability to push into sectors of our lives where it would previously not have been possible. Some of us may still remember Google Glass, a pair of digitised glasses that recorded all their surroundings, sent data to Google continuously, and displayed helpful information to the users on a screen within those glasses. After much public pushback, Google withdrew the product. However, this is an increasingly rare phenomenon of effective societal pushback against large financial interests.

In datafication and privacy, for example, the continued tracking and evaluation of all aspects of our lives wouldn't have been imaginable a decade or two ago. As a researcher, I observed this in my day-to-day work. When my colleagues in Oxford published the fact that Google and many other companies could collect data about users from nearly every Android app, this caused massive concern in 2018, when the study was released. The story even made it to the front page of the *Financial Times*, and Google issued a public statement that tried to cast doubt over those findings. This never happened again in our follow-up work, in which we showed that nothing had changed. The public has become resigned to the fact that privacy is lost online. More of this will be discussed in Chapter 7.

One of the most imminent technical changes might come through the increased capabilities of AI models. The release of ChatGPT in November 2022 made many in the software industry believe that an entirely new approach to computing might be upon us. While in the past, computing would follow clear instructions, LLMs, such as those underlying ChatGPT, take a randomised approach. This makes LLMs excel in an extensive range of tasks previously unthinkable for machines to solve. LLMs can now write poems, create photorealistic images, and serve as human-like assistants. In doing so, they give away an unprecedented air of autonomy and creativity, motivating many organisations to change gears completely. Legislators, like those in the EU, ushered in a range of novel legislation in response to all the potential, but so far rarely demonstrated, risks that LLMs may pose. Software companies are trying to add additional LLM-supported 'intelligence' to many parts of their software products. Microsoft was one of the quickest to release the 'Copilot' assistant that helps software engineers with programming, and by integrating ChatGPT into its Bing online search starting in February 2023. Google perceives ChatGPT as a potential threat to its main business model in online searches since ChatGPT arguably gives easier access to some information, but without showing any Google ads or sharing any data with the company. In response, multiple times, Google released immature AI assistants; therefore, creating even more doubts about the company's ability to keep up with AI innovation and save its online search (The Verge, 2024a; 2024b). Despite these concerns, Google's revenue from online search remains strong and consistent at the time of writing.

While other software companies have been rushing ahead, Apple has been taking a more measured approach. Only 1.5 years after ChatGPT's release, the company presented its vision of consumer AI, called 'Apple Intelligence'. Compared with competitors and in line with Apple's business strategy, Apple Intelligence puts a stronger emphasis on privacy. To this end, the company uses state-of-the-art encryption methods that promise to prevent Apple from ever seeing any user interactions with the AI. Furthermore, Apple Intelligence promises to be able to work across different apps and automate a significant amount of user interactions with their smartphones. Investors took Apple's announcements with great enthusiasm, sending the Apple stock to new record highs since then (BroadbandSearch, 2023).

The first iterations of the wide deployment of AI assistants, like Apple Intelligence, will likely disappoint. Moving forward, we may, however, see dramatic changes in how smartphones work. If AI assistants were successful, they would probably cement the dominance of Apple and Google in their respective ecosystems. After all, AI assistants aim to take over decision making from the user and thereby into the hands of the AI, that is, the hands of the

AI developer. They would collect even more data and be able to show more ads than they already do. In moving this way, the importance of individual apps may decline. Information would be sourced from a range of sources, including individual apps. Ideally, decision making would rarely show an app's interface anymore, but rather rush directly to the outcome of that decision. Pixar's film WALL-E may not have been fiction all along, having humans give vast decision making power to machines.

Given that Apple and Google dominate their respective ecosystems, the competitive threat from OpenAI and other smaller competitors will probably be limited to the domain of AI assistants. They have wider access to how the operating systems work and the platform defaults. This is also shown by Apple Intelligence, which, by default, uses an Apple AI model but might be changed to ChatGPT's, but only if the user so chooses. The extent to which Apple Intelligence is deeply integrated into Apple's operating systems, including macOS and iOS, further underlines the immense competitive disadvantages that OpenAI and others face in the app economy.

3.4 Unprecedented control over IT infrastructure, including AI and healthcare

The introduction of the app economy changed how computing works and, thereby, how many existing industries, for example, in media or gaming, operate. This is a usual feature of innovation and scientific progress and has been seen before, for instance, with the advent of personal computing or the automobile. What is different for the app economy, however, is that just two companies tightly control entry into the app economy. If companies want to offer apps to individuals, they must comply with the rules and standards set by Apple and Google. As we move into the AI era, this is unlikely to change, putting competitors like OpenAI and others at a significant competitive disadvantage in market access compared with Apple and Google. Moreover, the two companies have been building their footprints in the lucrative healthcare sector and will probably continue to do so. This is especially true since key innovations in the healthcare sector, not least AlphaFold, are driven by tech and AI expertise.

In light of these observations, in the following chapters, the focus will be on assessing the (systemic) risks arising from these two companies' decisions in the app economy.

The Legal Framework
of App Stores

Given the vast and varied influence of app ecosystems on our lives, one would expect that a range of targeted rules might exist for them, both to tame the practices of app store providers and those companies operating within the app ecosystem. However, few laws are explicitly aimed at app stores (Ó Fathaigh and van Hoboken, 2019; van Hoboken and Ó Fathaigh, 2021).

Readers who are already familiar with EU and US law as it pertains to app stores may want to proceed to the following chapter. The same might be true for readers not overly interested in the underlying legal issues. A deep understanding of the applicable laws is not required to understand the other chapters. In particular, while the concept of 'systemic risk' following the definition under the DSA is used as a lens for further analysis, this book does not aim to put exclusive focus on this law but instead develops a broader perspective on Apple and Google's market power in the app economy.

4.1 Federal Trade Commission: self-regulation in the US and the power of lobbying

In the US, besides the Department of Justice (DoJ), the Federal Trade Commission (FTC) is the leading enforcement agency for concerns around privacy and abuse of market power. In regulating digital platforms, the FTC has long pursued a strategy of self-regulation, in which it shied away from promoting new legislation and instead motivated private companies to restrict their conduct out of fear of even harsher legislation in case of no action. Given that the US Congress has been increasingly deadlocked over recent years, this fear has diminished. However, with a self-regulatory approach, the FTC was one of the first agencies to bring about tangible improvements to the conduct of app stores around 2013.

Motivated by concerns over smartphone data practices, the FTC solicited written submissions and hosted panel discussions. Ultimately, they published a 36-page report detailing their findings in 2013 (Federal Trade Commission, 2013). In this report, they found, among other aspects, that 'platforms have an important role to play in conveying privacy information to consumers' and made explicit recommendations as to what platforms should provide:

1. just-in-time permission pop-ups for access to sensitive data;
2. a privacy dashboard;
3. iconography for the collection of user data;
4. best developer practices;
5. information about the extent of app review;
6. compliance checks of apps even after their first release;
7. a do-not-track mechanism 'to prevent tracking by ad networks or other third parties as they navigate among apps on their phones'; and
8. an ability for app developers to link to a privacy policy directly on the app stores.

While these recommendations had no direct legal effect, Google and Apple implemented many of the suggestions. Both iOS and Android nowadays have permission pop-ups (1), privacy dashboards (2), privacy nutrition labels (3), and mandatory privacy policies on their app stores (8). These are positive improvements.

In addition, gaps remain, especially as they pertain to the underlying business model of Apple and Google in gaining higher shares of the smartphone market and developer revenues. For example, it took both companies a long time to implement more effective protections against app tracking (7). For example, as discussed in Chapter 7, Apple finally implemented a do-not-track mechanism in 2021 with the App Tracking Transparency (ATT) framework. The ATT allows individuals to refuse certain data collection without their consent by showing a pop-up. However, as of writing, similar protections remain absent from Android. Users can only restrict apps' access to the Android Advertising Identifier, which is hidden deeply in the settings and exempts many forms of tracking. At the same time, Apple's ATT remains limited and currently exempts tracking by Apple, as highlighted in my research (Kollnig et al, 2022b).

Meanwhile, Android has long disclosed the permissions, such as camera or calendar access, that apps can request and has complemented this with iconography (3). Apple did not do that until it introduced 'Privacy Nutrition Labels' in 2021, as shown in Figure 7.5. However, researchers have criticised both approaches as insufficient and often unhelpful for individuals (Felt et al, 2011; Van Kleek et al, 2018; Netzpolitik, 2022). Information about the extent of app review (5) remains poorly communicated to end users, and the compliance checks on apps (6) remain flawed (Kelley et al, 2013; Greene and Shilton, 2018).

It could be concluded that the FTC's self-regulatory approach has had mixed success in the context of app stores. There have been some changes to data practices on the surface. However, the agency did not bring about a more fundamental shift in the concentration of market power between Apple and Google. To date, app stores have not seen further action from the FTC nor the establishment of new targeted legislation by the US Congress.

It seems that the consensus around the suitability of the self-regulatory approach is slowly changing, across party lines. For example, in February 2022, the US Senate Judiciary Committee advanced a draft 'Open App Markets Act' with a strong 20–2 bipartisan vote. This bill would open up competition in the app economy and directly target Apple and Google's dominance. Similarly, the 'American Innovation and Choice Online Act' (AICOA) passed the House and Senate Committees on the Judiciary in 2021 and 2022, respectively. This law would, more generally, limit digital platforms' ability to engage in potentially anti-competitive conduct, such as self-preferencing.

In part due to intense lobbying, both bills have seen no further progress since (*Time*, 2022). According to Bloomberg, tech companies spent over $120 million on attack ads against the AICOA (Bloomberg, 2022b). Further, it was estimated that the total lobbying expenses of companies opposed to the AICOA exceeded more than $277 million between 2021 and 2022 (Public Citizen, 2022). As summarised by Tim Wu 'Everyone knows that lobbying works' (Wu, 2018). After analysing 1,779 different policy issues, this statement was backed up with empirical evidence: 'economic elites and organised groups representing business interests have substantial independent impacts on US government policy, while average citizens and mass-based interest groups have little or no independent influence' (Gilens and Page, 2014). The relative lack of influence is partly rooted in the fact that it's usually much more challenging to unite individual citizens behind one political cause rather than a few select companies (Wu, 2018). This makes it arguably even more important to assess the immense market power of a few tech companies in the app economy, as attempted in this book.

4.2 GDPR: technology-neutral regulation in the EU

In the EU, there too, long existed no regulation that was explicitly targeted at app stores. Instead, there has traditionally been a desire to regulate the technical space in a technology-neutral way. The most prominent example is the widely debated GDPR. Rather than being prescriptive as to how data protection needs to be achieved, the GDPR, in Article 5, stipulates a range of high level principles that must be followed during the processing of personal data (that is, data that relates to individuals):

- lawfulness, fairness, and transparency
- purpose limitation
- data minimisation
- accuracy
- storage limitation
- integrity and confidentiality
- accountability

The primary responsibility for implementing those principles in software lies with the data controller, which determines the 'purposes and means of the processing of personal data' (Article 4(7) GDPR). Commonly, the controller will be the publisher of the mobile app in question. However, the GDPR (Article 26) also entails the concept of 'joint controllership', in which more than one party acts as the controller. This concept has proved particularly controversial in modern IT systems, which often include components from dozens, if not hundreds, of different contributors. Here, it can be highly unclear who actually determines the purposes and means of personal data processing. A series of case law of the Court of Justice of the European Union (CJEU), including Wirtschaftsakademie (2018), Jehovah's Witnesses (2018), and Fashion ID (2019); therefore, has been clarifying the concept of controllership.

For example, in the Wirtschaftsakademie case (visualised in Figure 4.1), a German data protection authority fined the company Wirtschaftsakademie Schleswig-Holstein GmbH for operating a Facebook fan page without adequately informing page visitors that their data would be processed. In

Figure 4.1: An illustration of the Wirtschaftsakademie case

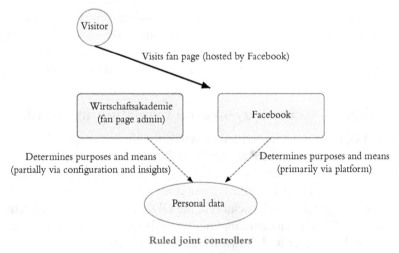

response, Wirtschaftsakademie argued that they were not responsible but rather that responsibility lay with Facebook. After all, Wirtschaftsakademie was not directly processing any personal data from visitors. The company did, however, profit from this data through Facebook Insights, where it could monitor site statistics, such as the number of unique page visitors over time. It also had a range of configuration choices about the data collection in question, including setting up the fan page to begin with. In light of this, the CJEU ruled that Wirtschaftsakademie and Facebook jointly determine the means and purposes of data processing, albeit for different parts of the personal data processing. This shows how, in practice, the legal responsibility of controllers extends to those parts of personal data processing that they influence. Sometimes, this influence might be large, as is the case for Facebook, designing and operating a whole social media platform; sometimes it might be comparatively smaller, as was the case for Wirtschaftsakademie, merely operating a Facebook fan page. In this way, gaps in responsibility for personal data processing are prevented.

In the future, as IT systems become more and more complex, the concept of controllership will probably evolve further and become ever more important. As regards data practices of apps on app stores, it may even entail the providers of app stores themselves, who commonly facilitate the processing of personal data by other controllers in mobile apps. Under the speculative assumption that Apple and Google had to fulfill more controller obligations in their respective app ecosystems, this could have drastic consequences for the status quo in those ecosystems. Take the principle of 'transparency'. As alluded to previously in this book, studying app ecosystems remains challenging and requires highly sophisticated technical approaches. Indeed, in some of my latest research, over 100 academic papers were reviewed, and many deliberate techniques employed by Apple and Google were identified to make their app ecosystems less transparent and accountable (Kollnig and Shadbolt, 2023). Hence, the transparency obligations under the GDPR might imply that Apple and Google must remove some of the hurdles relating to the transparency of data processing in apps. The other principles of the GDPR might have similar far-reaching implications for app stores, but have not been realised either. More of this will be discussed in Chapter 7.

While an ambitious law, the GDPR currently struggles with enforcement in practice. One reason is the law's relatively new, principle-driven and technology-neutral nature, necessitating lengthy clarification of the key terms in the courts. Another reason is the decentralised enforcement of the GDPR by the data protection authorities in the 27 EU member states. Many tech companies have strategically set up their EU headquarters in Ireland. All complaints against the GDPR violations of these tech companies must then, under the rules of the GDPR, be consulted with the Irish data protection authority. This authority, however, is known to be understaffed, industry friendly, and slow working, which has been one of the key roadblocks to effective enforcement of GDPR principles vis-à-vis tech companies (Irish Council for Civil Liberties, 2021). In fact, underfunding is an issue shared by many data protection authorities across the EU (Massé, 2020), holding back enforcement.

As a result of these challenges, even many years after the law was adopted in 2016, basic definitions under the GDPR are still being clarified and challenged in court. For example, Meta, the parent company of Facebook, was recently found to violate the GDPR by relying on, with the support of the Irish data protection, 'contract necessity' as a legal ground for data collection. Facebook had been arguing that its users had signed up for Facebook to receive personalised advertising. If this were true, Facebook would not have to rely on one of the other five legal grounds besides contract, such as user consent. Interestingly, Facebook had used consent as the legal ground until the GDPR came into force in May 2018, and then changed it overnight, as if its users had all suddenly changed their minds. In response to the ruling, Facebook has now changed back to consent. Users can now choose between paying for an ad-free subscription or giving 'consent' to seeing Facebook ads and having their data used for these ads. However, whether such a solution passes the high bar for consent under GDPR, which, among other aspects, must be 'freely given', remains to be seen. It is likely that, again, this matter will be settled in a few years before the EU's highest court.

Overall, the GDPR remains a relatively new law with limited clarification by the courts and scarce enforcement by the responsible authorities. It struggles to have tangible effects on the practices of app store providers. The efficacy of the GDPR is hampered by its technology neutral nature. While the EU once intended to clarify the exact technical implications of the GDPR with an ePrivacy Regulation (lex specialis), these efforts have stalled due to disagreement between the EU member states. In the meantime, the outdated ePrivacy Directive from 2002 takes up this function, even though this law was drafted long before data invasive smartphones became widespread. As it stands, it does not seem likely that these disagreements will be resolved and that the GDPR may take a more substantial role in regulating Apple and Google's dominance in the app economy.

4.3 DSA, DMA, and other EU platform laws

Given the vast dominance of a few digital platforms, countries around the globe have been working on enacting new legislation in response.

4.3.1 Platform-to-business relations

One of the first initiatives was the EU's 2019 Regulation on promoting fairness and transparency for business users of online intermediation services, also known as the Regulation on Platform-to-Business Relations (P2BR). This regulation addresses the power imbalance between the providers of online marketplaces (such as Amazon or app stores) and the businesses operating and relying on those marketplaces. Among the obligations on platforms under the law is a need to give 15 days' notice before any changes to terms and conditions (Article 3), protections against unjustified suspensions or restrictions of business accounts (for example, Articles 4, 11, and 14), and mandatory disclosures about platform self-preferencing (Article 7). Overall, this law brings some improvements for businesses operating on app stores but mainly aims at traditional e-commerce platforms, such as Amazon and contains no specific measures for app stores (Ó Fathaigh and van Hoboken, 2019).

As mentioned in the Introduction, in late 2022, EU lawmakers adopted two more notable new pieces of legislation for digital markets: the DMA and DSA. The laws pursue similar aims but with different strategies. In case of non-compliance, companies can be charged up to 20 per cent (DMA) or 6 per cent (DSA) of their annual global turnover, respectively.

4.3.2 Competition and DMA

The DMA tries to ensure 'for all businesses, contestable and fair markets in the digital sector across the Union where gatekeepers are present' (Article 1 DMA), and thereby update EU competition law for the age of digital platforms. It breaks with the EU's previous technology-neutral and principle-based approach to technology regulation. Instead, it includes a list of explicit (but with varying levels of detail) obligations for gatekeepers. As such, the EU has been trying to shift from an ex post to an ex ante regulatory regime. The specific obligations concern interoperability between competing services (for example, messaging apps), data access for business users, and restrictions on platform self-preferencing.

Among the obligations that relate specifically to app stores are:

- the requirement to allow end-users to uninstall pre-installed default apps and switch to alternative apps easily;
- an obligation on gatekeepers not to require end or business users to use a browser engine or a payment service;
- restrictions on the tracking of users outside the core platform without users' effective consent; and
- the ability for users to install apps from outside the app store (sideloading).

There are some early reports on some successes of the DMA. For example, due to the obligation to allow the uninstallation of pre-installed apps, Apple must now allow the installation of alternative browsers, including browser engines,[1] and actively ask users whether they want to use a non-Apple web browser on iOS devices. In response, alternative browser makers, such as DuckDuckGo or Vivaldi, reported an uptick in market share on iOS (Reuters, 2024b). Counterintuitively, however, the choice screen is shown when users first open the Safari browser, which could be an abuse of Apple's market power and is being investigated by the European Commission (European Commission, 2024).

Further, in response to the requirement to allow alternative browser engines, Apple briefly banned web apps on iOS, claiming that it would be a disproportionate effort to extend alternative browser engines to web apps. However, following pressure from the European Commission, Apple ended up reverting this decision again. Web apps are somewhat critical for Apple's iOS revenues because they offer an alternative to so-called native apps. Native apps are those apps distributed via Apple and Google's app stores, over which these two companies have exclusive control. Meanwhile, web apps can be downloaded on any phone via a web browser without having to pay any commission on transactions to Apple or Google. The fact that Apple must now enable sideloading and alternative app stores probably further encourages the company to act against alternative ways of app distribution. Further, while sideloading is now possible, app developers will have to pay a Core Technology Fee (CTF) to Apple, regardless of the distribution channel. The CTF amounts to €0.50 and must be paid by the app developer for every app install exceeding 1 million installs over a year (Apple, 2024a). The CTF does not apply to web apps because these are websites and, therefore, more difficult to police by Apple.

Overall, Apple seems to have reacted with relative fury to the DMA. The law arguably poses more significant threats to its vertically integrated iOS model than Android. Thus, Apple has a stronger incentive to try to comply to the minimum extent legally necessary or delay compliance as long as possible. This is a common tactic in compliance with technology laws. As long as there's no threat of enforcement and sanctions, companies will not comply.

It remains to be seen what the exact outcomes of the DMA will be. There is a risk that it's too little, too late and that the DMA may struggle to keep up with rapid technological changes. Compared with other EU tech laws, such as the GDPR, the DMA is less technology-neutral and principle-driven, and describes in more detail what gatekeepers must fulfil their obligations. Some of those obligations are relatively broad, while others are specific. This will pose challenges in translating the broader provisions into practice and keeping the more specific provisions aligned with the state-of-the-art in digital technologies.

The European Commission has ways to update these obligations (Articles 12 and 19). However, according to common economic opinion, intervention is most effective before a market has 'tipped' towards dominance by a single gatekeeper (Dubé et al, 2007; Wu, 2018). The DMA might end up stifling innovation and competition in some regards and might negatively affect smaller non-gatekeeper companies (Portuese, 2021; ExchangeWire, 2024; Hoffmann et al, 2024).

Besides the EU and the US, in the domain of competition law, one of the most active nations has been the UK's Competition and Markets Authority (CMA). They, for example, created one of the most comprehensive reports on dominance in the app economy (Competition and Markets Authority, 2022b). In response to the findings from their 356-page report, the CMA started further investigation of Apple's potential abuse of dominance in the markets for browser and cloud engines and initiated an investigation into Google's payment policies on the Play Store. The CMA has recently received an expanded mandate to intervene ex ante against dominance in digital markets through the new Digital Markets, Competition and Consumers Bill. Meanwhile, in June 2024, Japan adopted DMA-style obligations for app stores, dubbed the 'Act on Promotion of Competition for Specified Smartphone Software'. It remains to be seen what implications these laws will have.

Overall, there seems to be a global consensus that Apple and Google should not be allowed to self-preference their own digital services in the app economy and, within reason, enable their competitors to operate within this economy.

4.3.3 Consumer protection and DSA

The DSA tries to enhance EU consumer protection law. One of the primary motivations for introducing this law was concern about the impacts of social media on society, including disinformation, hate speech, inadequate content moderation, and the widespread use of algorithmic systems by online platforms (AI). The law widely applies to online services, small and large. However, the most stringent obligations under the law apply to Very Large Online Platforms (VLOPs) and Very Large Online Search Engines (VLOSEs). These are online platforms and search engines that have more than 45 million monthly active users in the EU (representing about 10 per cent of the population). According to the European Commission, there were two VLOSEs (Bing and Google) and 23 VLOPs in their first designation of status in April 2023, as of December 2024. Among the VLOPs were Facebook, Instagram, the Amazon Store, Google Maps, Wikipedia, and the two app stores by Google and Apple.

The VLOPs and VLOSEs face a range of obligations. Some of the most stringent ones arise from the need to conduct regular assessments of 'systemic risks' posed by the platform (Article 34), the need to put in place reasonable, proportionate and effective mitigation measures (Article 35 DSA), and the need to give researchers access to platform data to allow them to study systemic risks facilitated by the platform (Article 40). As mentioned before, the systemic risks include:

- the dissemination of illegal content;
- impacts on the exercise of fundamental rights (in particular, the fundamental rights to human dignity, respect for private and family life, the protection of personal data, freedom of expression and information, including the freedom and pluralism of the media, non-discrimination, respect for the rights of the child and a high level of consumer protection);
- negative effects on the democratic process; and
- impediments to health and well-being (Article 34(1) DSA).

In conducting risk assessments, the providers of platforms need to consider, in particular, the design of their recommender systems and any other relevant algorithmic system; their content moderation systems; the applicable terms and conditions and their enforcement; systems for selecting and presenting advertisements; and data related practices of the provider (Article 34(2) DSA). The explicit mention of these considerations highlights that the law was not tailored to app stores but was mainly drafted with social media and e-commerce platforms in mind. The recommendations are strongly focused on the use of algorithmic systems, which, compared with social media, play a relatively small role in app stores and operating systems.

Regardless of the intent, the risk assessments and mitigation measures have an extensive scope. They clarify that platforms play a key role in societies and, therefore, are responsible for reducing harm. This clarification is important because fundamental rights, such as the protection of privacy and personal data, do not usually apply directly to private companies but rather aim to protect private parties from the state (Kokott and Sobotta, 2013). If done well, this approach promises to improve the protection of individuals on a great scale.

To fulfil the lofty ambitions behind the DSA, we will need enforcement of the laws that keep pace with the technical and legal expertise of the platforms. Unlike the GDPR, the regulation is centralised with the European Commission (rather than the data protection authorities of the 27 EU member states) and promises to improve enforcement. As for the funding of the regulatory oversight, the DSA embraces an innovative approach, in which platforms can be charged up to 0.05 per cent of their worldwide annual net income to support the law's enforcement. This tries to address the problem of underfunding of responsible authorities, which still holds back GDPR enforcement.

The broad scope of the provisions also opens them up to attack. Because many harms posed by platforms might be interpreted as a systemic risk, this creates a risk for regulatory overreach. This, in response, might motivate a narrow interpretation of the law by courts in practice and allow companies to engage in the same 'compliance theatre' as with the GDPR. In the GDPR, many companies started adopting cookie banners, even though the GDPR does not mention cookies. The underlying data practices remained widely unchanged, as found in my research. Before and after the introduction of the GDPR, about 40 per cent of Android apps could share data with Meta/ Facebook and 90 per cent with Alphabet/Google (Kollnig et al, 2021b). Despite high hopes, the GDPR did not manage to tangibly make many digital industries overcome their reliance on large amounts of sensitive data.

The greatest risk to the law might lie in the nature of European regulation. Similar to the GDPR, we should expect a wealth of legal challenges to the applicability of these laws and the increasing obligations on providers of online platforms, including app stores.

In Section 5.3, more will be discussed about how Article 40 of the DSA can be used to access platform data from the two app stores.

4.4 Enforcement through courts in the EU and the US

New targeted legislation is still in its infancy; however, app stores face scrutiny over existing laws, such as consumer protection and competition laws.

4.4.1 Europe

In the EU, the European Commission is the primary authority that handles cross-border competition law violations. It previously brought two cases against Google.

In the Google Android case, the European Commission found that Google illegally abused its market position vis-à-vis the producers of Android smartphones (also called Original Equipment Manufacturers (OEMs)) and imposed a fine of €4.3 billion on Google in July 2018. The company appealed the decisions before the CJEU, which reduced the fine to €4.125 billion in 2022. In its ruling, the Court confirmed that Google has a monopoly on licensed mobile operating systems. This is because Apple does not license its iOS software, and because the open source nature of Android is not sufficient to remedy this situation. This underlines the fact that Google and Apple operate on different operating systems and that Google exerts strict control over Android despite it being open source.

In the Google Shopping case, the European Commission found in June 2017 that Google had abused its dominant position in online search by illegally promoting its price comparison website over other competitors and imposed a €2.42 billion fine on Google. Again, Google appealed the Commission's decision at the CJEU. However, the Court ruled to uphold the fine in November 2021.

The two previous Google cases show that, in principle, competition law already provides protections against the abuse of market dominance by large online platforms. Under EU competition law, the European Commission can impose a fine of up to 10 per cent of the overall annual turnover (Article 23 of EU Regulation 01/2003). It may also impose any behavioural or structural remedies that are proportionate to the infringement committed and necessary to bring the infringement effectively to an end (Article 7 of EU Regulation 01/2003). These structural remedies might go as far as ordering the break-up of a company. Indeed, this is what the European Commission ordered Google to do in June 2023 in the context of its online advertising business. However, this new case is ongoing.

Despite the immense powers under EU competition law, serious practical challenges remain. Both previously completed competition cases against Google took years for the European Commission to develop and then for the CJEU to settle (about 4 years each). Further, conducting these cases remains challenging. The Google Android and Google Shopping case focused on somewhat visible aspects of the digital economy, that is, prominent self-preferencing of Google services and pre-installing of Google services on all Android handsets. These previous cases have struggled to untangle the abuse of power underneath the surface. The new case against Google Advertising presents a change away from this past scheme, but also requires significant amounts of transatlantic efforts. DoubleClick, which sits at the heart of this case, was acquired by Google in 2008 and is only now being challenged.

Previous competition fines imposed seemed to do little to remedy the situation. In 2022, Google had a revenue of $224.47 billion and was vastly profitable. The UK competition authority, analysing the dominance of Google and Facebook, found that 'the profitability of both Google and Facebook has been well above what is required to reward investors with a fair return for many years' and that they 'would expect these excess profits to be shared more freely with consumers in a more competitive market' (Competition and Markets Authority, 2020). In other words, Google is much more profitable than other firms, partly because it owns so little fixed capital as an internet business compared with traditional firms and partly because it is likely to be anti-competitive.

In March 2024, the European Commission fined Apple €1.8 billion over its anti-competitive practices towards competitors in music streaming, such as Spotify. Therefore, the Commission concluded an investigation that started in 2020, following Spotify's complaint over Apple's practice in 2019. This, again, shows the long time that traditional competition complaints take. The fine is not final, and Apple will likely appeal it, promising further delays.

Given the challenges in bringing cases against large platforms, the EU has now changed to more direct regulation of digital platforms through the DSA and DMA, as discussed earlier in this chapter.

4.4.2 United States

In the US, a notable case is Epic Games v. Apple Inc. (2020), as discussed in chapter 4.3. In this case, the Northern District of California investigated potential monopolistic behaviour by Apple. In her ruling, the judge largely sided with Apple but identified some anti-competitive conduct on Apple's part. She ordered Apple to allow app developers to inform app users of alternative payment methods, which the company previously denied through its App Store policies. Apple and Epic Games both appealed, but the Supreme Court eventually refused to hear the case in 2023.

Another important, ongoing case is *In re Google Play Store Antitrust Litigation*, in which four groups of plaintiffs, including Epic Games, allege that Google maintains an illegal monopoly in Android. They argue, among other aspects, that Google has a monopoly in the Android app store market, abuses its privileged market position vis-à-vis app developers and phone manufacturers, and makes it too difficult for end users to install alternative app stores. As such, these concerns mirror those that are being addressed in the EU through competition cases and new platform law.

In overseeing cases against tech companies, the US courts face difficult trade-offs. Clear concerns arise from the current practices of tech companies, which need some form of legal deterrent. However, tech companies also contribute massively to the US economy.

A recent Supreme Court judgement brought up this balance between promoting innovation and protecting against the abuse of dominance. The Court decided in 2021 on the case Google v Oracle, which had been running since August 2010. Oracle, which had acquired Sun for $7.4 billion in the year before (April 2009), sued Google for using Sun components in the Android operating system. Specifically, Google copied about 11,000 lines of source code from Sun's Java framework for Android. Java was a popular programming language; therefore, many software developers already knew how to use it. This is why Google made Java the default language for Android, as discussed in Chapter 2. To this end, Google only copied a small part of Java's source code, so-called application programming interfaces (APIs), to make it easier for developers to adapt their existing Java code for Android and start building new apps quickly.

The Supreme Court found that Google's actions were covered by the fair use exemption under US copyright law, which seeks to promote transformative innovations. Because of Android's 'transformative' nature in creating a new market for a new kind of smartphone, Google was permitted to copy Oracle's code. The open source nature of Android helped developers build innovative new apps based on new and ground-breaking approaches to personal computing. According to the US Supreme Court, this approach remains subject to protection.

Finally, on 5 August 2024, US District Judge Amit Mehta ruled in the United States of America v. Google case that Google has an illegal monopoly in online search and advertising. One of the potential remedies that has been discussed much is the break-up of Google, particularly the divestment of the Android platform. Chapter 11, which deals with how to respond to Apple and Google's dominance, will pick up this idea. The case will take many more years to be litigated in the US courts, potentially up to the Supreme Court. A final decision is not expected before 2026.

4.5 Limited, technology-neutral legal obligations

The two large app store providers face relatively few explicit legal obligations. Where they exist, they tend to focus on economic harms but rarely on wider societal ones. Legislators have traditionally aimed to be technology-neutral, which makes it difficult to implement and enforce the legal norms.

In the EU, the P2BR has a broad scope for online platforms. The DSA is very open-ended and only engages with app stores in passing. The regular risk assessments and transparency obligations, including data access for researchers, are promising. However, there is a risk that both will remain relatively light-touch compliance exercises with limited teeth. Transparency and risk assessment, by themselves, are unlikely to weigh against strong economic incentives on the part of the platforms. Overall, it may take a long time for the DSA to have meaningful effects on the practices of app stores. However, if they do, these effects could be broad and beyond narrow economic considerations due to the DSA's emphasis on systemic risks.

Compared with the DSA, the DMA is more targeted at app stores and even has explicit obligations for them. Unlike the DSA, these obligations are mainly aimed at anti-competitive business practices, such as all forms of self-preferencing of the platform. This focus on economic harms may struggle to capture the broader non-economic harms (such as privacy (Chapter 7) and health (Chapter 8)), which are the main subject of this book.

The EU's enactment of the DSA and DMA underlines that it is not the state, as it has been traditionally, but increasingly private companies that play an essential role in protecting fundamental rights and freedoms. If the platforms do not live up to this task, then this can create 'systemic risks', which could pose significant harm to the functioning of our democracies. Therefore, the rest of this book will take the concept of 'systemic risks', the cornerstone of the DSA, as a lens to analyse the current practices of app store providers critically. In light of the absence of any targeted regulation, this analysis will eventually be used to develop an adequate regulatory response.

Some of the most significant challenges to Google and Apple arise from the ongoing court proceedings based on established bodies of law. This also raises the question of whether new laws have been necessary in the first place, or whether one should have devoted more resources earlier to enforcing those existing laws.

A core theme across all the current initiatives is the struggle of the law to keep up with exponentially changing technologies. Court proceedings usually take years, and the same is true for enacting new laws. Laws such as the DMA are trying to move from ex post to ex ante remedies. However, these laws also risk being stuck in the past or struggling to be translated into practice. Some of the DMA's remedies are rather specific. They cannot easily be changed as digital technologies evolve. As a result, supposed ex ante legal remedies may be ex post remedies in disguise.

These challenges in keeping up with the law are particularly relevant, given that we're currently witnessing the emergence of a new approach to computing. This has been brought on us by the creation of advanced AI models, as first popularised by OpenAI's ChatGPT. These AI models synthesise decades of human knowledge and can reason upon it, albeit in a somewhat limited capacity.

The new 'Apple Intelligence' framework takes this further and practically demonstrates how AI may revolutionise computing. It strives to automate users' interactions with their phones and replace them with fewer, or even speech-based, interactions. The Apple Vision Pro gives another example of how virtual reality (VR) glasses might replace regular phones and desktop computers with a sophisticated virtual environment embedded in our surroundings. As Chapters 3 and 9 discuss, Apple and Google are in a brilliant position to translate their dominance in the smartphone economy into dominance in VR and AI.

One can only imagine how computing may change even further in the coming years and may deviate from how the law perceives these key technologies. As it stands, it seems that the power of these technological gatekeepers will increase further. The law may have a hard time keeping up.

App Research with Technical and Legal Methods

While much previous research on digital platforms exists, app ecosystems usually only get analysed in passing. A key reason for this is that much platform scholarship derives from disciplines that are not used to working with code artefacts, such as mobile apps, and instead focus on social media (Facebook, Twitter, and TikTok) or e-commerce (Amazon) platforms. As a result of this absence of study and discussion, few laws exist that are explicitly targeted at app ecosystems. This leaves the companies' control over our smartphone-dependent societies relatively unbridled.

Over the past decade, two main methods have emerged for analysing mobile apps: dynamic and static analysis. Recently, the study of apps' privacy policies and privacy nutrition labels (which all apps must provide) has become popular. However, the policies and the labels are self-disclosed by app publishers, tend to be incomplete, and provide limited or misleading insights into apps' actual data practices. An overview of the typical steps for analysing mobile apps is shown in Figure 5.1.

During my PhD research at Oxford (building on previous research in my research group), I developed a complete end-to-end solution for this process.[1] Since the needs of researchers can differ from my own research needs, and because the tooling for app analysis quickly becomes outdated, this chapter will dive into the engineering and design of app analysis tooling in more detail.

Importantly, other approaches exist that allow the analysis of other aspects of apps that are not covered in this chapter. This relates particularly to human factors methods that study how individuals use mobile apps (for example, through cognitive walkthrough, observation, interviews, and prototypes) and to reverse engineering. Because there is much overlap with other disciplines, this book will not discuss these techniques in detail.

Sometimes, rather than collecting data yourself, paying for data from data providers might be the most straightforward approach. 42matters is an example of one of them. It provides detailed data about apps across various

Figure 5.1: Overview of the usual process for app analysis

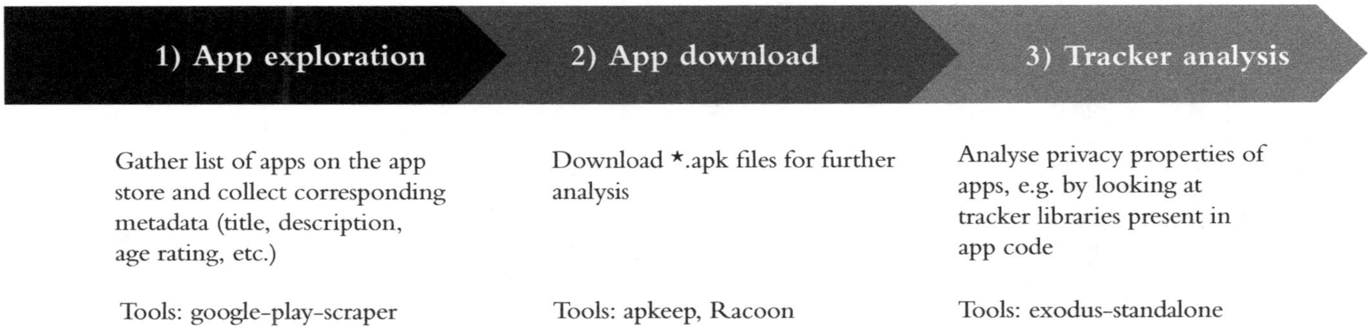

1) App exploration

Gather list of apps on the app store and collect corresponding metadata (title, description, age rating, etc.)

Tools: google-play-scraper

2) App download

Download *.apk files for further analysis

Tools: apkeep, Racoon

3) Tracker analysis

Analyse privacy properties of apps, e.g. by looking at tracker libraries present in app code

Tools: exodus-standalone

Source: Kollnig and Shadbolt (2023)

app stores, spanning many years. However, these data providers mainly aim at commercial organisations interested in monitoring their competitors and tend to serve different needs than those of academic researchers. They also charge very high fees for data access (for example, about €15,000 for full data access in the case of 42matters).

The need to manually collect data may be mitigated by the adoption of the DSA in 2022. As it stands, it provides researchers with access to information about apps on the app stores but no access to the actual app packages. However, the actual app packages are usually necessary for the in-depth analysis of apps' practices. This will be discussed in more detail later in this chapter.

As a means of warning, this chapter will provide some computer code to illustrate how data about apps can be collected and analysed. It is not expected that every reader can understand this code. If in doubt, these parts can be skipped, or the help of a befriended tech nerd can be sought.

5.1 App exploration, selection, and download

The first and arguably most important step for analysing apps is usually the selection of apps on the app stores, the subsequent selection of apps, and the downloading of app metadata. It is possible to access (some of) this data through Article 40 of the DSA. This chapter first explains how to obtain access without it and then dives into experiences with the DSA.

5.1.1 Tooling and set-up

For all three steps, good, ready-to-use tooling exists. The development of the most commonly used tooling is led by the independent app developer, Facundo Olano:

- iOS: https://github.com/facundoolano/app-store-scraper
- Android https://github.com/facundoolano/google-play-scraper

The operation of these tools requires a working setup of Node.js and some familiarity with coding in JavaScript. After installing Node.js, the relevant library needs to be installed by running the install command in a terminal:

```
npm install app-store-scraper google-play-scraper
```

Next, one needs to start Node.js (for example, by running the command 'node' from a terminal). Basic information about each app, provided by its identifier, can then be retrieved via the command:

```
// Android
var gplay = require('google-play-scraper');
gplay.app({appId: 'com.spotify.music'})
.then(console.log, console.log);
// iOS
var store = require('app-store-scraper');
store.app({appId: 'com.spotify.client'}).then(console.log).catch(console.log);
```

Under the hood, the two tools retrieve the requested information from the respective app store webpage. For example, for the Play Store, the Google-Play-Scraper library opens the webpage[2] and extracts all relevant metadata from that website. It is important to note that both libraries provide a range of further functionality whose explanation is beyond the scope of this book.

5.1.2 App exploration and selection

The next step aims to generate a list of apps for further study and analysis.

Exploration can be skipped if one is only interested in analysing the top apps on the app stores, for example, the most downloaded or highest-grossing apps. For this case, both app stores provide data about the top apps for each genre (for example, Productivity, Games, and News). The number of apps is, however, limited to around 100. The complete list of genres is inconsistent between the App Store (24 genres and 18 subgenres for games) and the Play Store (36 genres and 17 subgenres for games). The fact that there are so many subgenres for games highlights how much mobile gaming contributes to the app economy.

```
gplay.list({
    category: gplay.category.PRODUCTIVITY,
    collection: gplay.collection.TOP_FREE,
    num: 50
})
.then(console.log, console.log);
```

Only focusing on the top apps brings several advantages. The data collection is relatively simple to perform and only requires a few lines of code and a little bit of storage. One also covers a considerable proportion of the digital realities of most app users. Most of us use the same apps and spend the most time on them, such as YouTube, Google Chrome, and Spotify.

While some top apps stay in the charts for many years, there is much movement among the top apps. Many apps only have a lifetime of a few months and will quickly lose users once their temporary popularity has passed. Hence, if one only studies the top apps, one may run into challenges related to reproducibility. The make-up of the top apps is changing quickly, which makes re-running the same study in the future more difficult. Large-scale studies do not suffer from these problems because they have greater statistical robustness. Hence, it has become common in the technical community to focus on a four-digit number of apps as the bare minimum (for example, 1,000 apps or more).

If one wants to analyse a larger number of apps, then one can either: (1) choose the top apps from more genres; or (2) explore the totality of apps on the app stores in a systematic fashion.

Regarding the latter, two main strategies exist. One strategy is to start with a list of 'seed' app IDs and fetch the information for the apps related to each of these IDs, including the app IDs of the 'similar' apps as indicated on the app stores. Subsequently, this step is repeated with the newly identified apps, now being part of the 'seed' apps. Sample code would be the following:

```
(async () => {
    to_visit = ['com.spotify.music', 'com.microsoft.teams', 'com.amazon.mShop.android.
shopping']; // seed
    visited = [];
    while (to_visit.length > 0) {
    let appId = to_visit.pop();
    console.log(appId);
    visited.push(appId);
    suggestions = await gplay.similar({appId: appId});
    suggestions.forEach(app => {
    if (!visited.includes(app.appId))
    to_visit.push(app.appId);
    });
    }
})()
```

Another commonly used approach is to leverage the autocomplete functionality of the app search of the respective app stores (Viennot et al, 2014; Binns et al, 2018). In the first step, one creates a list of 'seed' search terms, for example, all possible combinations of lowercase characters up to a length of three characters. These seeds are then fed into the search algorithm of the respective app stores, which returns a list of apps and their IDs.

5.1.3 Metadata, including app reviews, ranks, and privacy information

After generating a list of apps and their IDs for further analysis, one can move on to gathering the metadata, such as app title, description, reviews, and rank. Some of this information might have already been obtained using the existing tooling during the app exploration. However, there is a good chance that one might have missed downloading some information in the earlier analysis that may later become relevant. Because it is difficult to travel back in time and to complete missing information about apps, it is usually wise to err on the side of completeness of the dataset. More data is usually better.

For example, apps come with hundreds of reviews, which might be interesting for research that studies users' experiences with apps (Wang et al, 2021). Other researchers have been interested in studying the ranks of apps, which can be obtained from both app stores, albeit only to a limited extent (Roma and Ragaglia, 2016). An increasing number of research studies have also looked into apps' privacy policies (Harkous et al, 2018; Zimmeck et al, 2019) and privacy nutrition labels (Kelley et al, 2009).

The storage of the metadata might happen in JSON files or a sophisticated database, such as a PostgreSQL database, as in my PhD research.

5.1.4 App download and installation

After selecting a list of apps of interest and saving their metadata for future analysis, the next step is to download the apps. To avoid account bans, one should never use one's personal app store account during that process.

If the set of apps of interest is small (for example, fewer than 50), it might be enough to download these apps manually from the Google Play or Apple App Store on a testing smartphone. However, this approach only allows for limited reproducibility and re-analysis in the future. Instead, it is good practice to download apps so that they can be archived outside of a physical phone, for example, on a hard drive or dedicated server.

5.1.4.1 App Store

The download of iOS apps has traditionally been highly challenging. Given the highly restricted nature of the iOS ecosystem, few tools were available. This slowly started to change throughout my PhD. In the absence of alternatives, I developed a download tool that relies on running a specific version of iTunes (version 12.6.5.3) on a Windows computer.[3] A more recent option is ipatool, which allows the easy downloading of apps. This is another command line tool that is operated via a terminal. It relies on a working App Store account and an initial login via two-factor authentication.

The result of the download is an '.ipa' file that can be installed via various tools, for example, the command-line tool 'ideviceinstaller' that exists for all desktop operating systems.

For small-scale research, an approach to download '.ipa' files without the need to use a command-line tool is to use the previously mentioned iTunes version 12.6.5.3 on a Windows computer. With this program, apps can be downloaded directly from the App Store and stored in a local app library, similar to a music library. The '.ipa' files are saved alongside music, videos, and other files in a central location in the filesystem.

5.1.4.2 Play Store

Downloading Android apps from the Google Play Store has become more complicated in recent years. Google is trying, via various methods, to restrict the automated download of apps. Among other aspects, Google, unlike Apple, checks the precise HTTPS handshake when contacting its servers. If this handshake does not match what is expected on an Android device, the Google Play Store servers refuse to communicate. Another approach is Google's roll-out of split '.apk' files, which, if enabled, can create dozens of different versions for a single app. These mainly serve to reduce the size of app downloads, but also make it more challenging to test different configurations of apps. More generally, Google has constantly changed its measures against downloading. Despite that, Android has traditionally received more attention from the research community. There are many tools that promise downloading from the Google Play Store, but are out-of-date and broken.

The most reliable current tools are Racoon and apkeep. The latter was developed by the Electronic Frontier Foundation. Rather than only allowing users to download apps from the Google Play Store, it also supports several alternatives, including APKPure and the F-Droid Store. It might, however, be the case that these alternative stores do not provide the same version as Google Play. Hence, apps should be downloaded using apkeep, such as with the following terminal command:

```
apkeep -a [app ID] -d google-play -o split_apk=true -u '[Google Play email]' -p
[Google Play password]
```

The split_apk command additionally makes sure that the complete app is downloaded.

For small-scale research, an approach to download the '.apk' file without the need to use a command-line tool is the use of the Aurora App Store. This app is unavailable from the Google Play Store and must be downloaded from the free and open-source F-Droid store. Aurora allows the straightforward download of '.apk' files from the Play Store.

(Split) apks can be installed on a connected real device with the adb install-multiple [appId]/*.apk terminal command, provided that all apk files are put in a [appId] folder and that the terminal is located in the folder above that folder.

5.2 App analysis with technical methods

5.2.1 Dynamic analysis for in-depth insights

Dynamic analysis is a common way to analyse apps downloaded from the Apple App Store or Google Play Store. In contrast to static analysis, this approach runs an app of interest on a real device to observe its real world behaviour. This approach is relatively easy to use and gives quality insights into apps' behaviour, but cannot easily be scaled across large numbers of apps due to the reliance on real devices.

Dynamic analysis has a long history in the technical literature. Early research focused on modifying the operating system to observe what was going on inside the system. As discussed in more detail in Section 8.4.2, TaintDroid was a modified Android version published in 2010. It allowed the monitoring of data flows within the operating system (Enck et al, 2010). This approach identified sources of sensitive data (for example, the camera, phone contacts, and device identifiers) and sinks (for example, the file system and network requests). All data that emerged from a source was labelled, monitored as it traversed through the Android system, and flagged if it reached one of the sinks.

Meanwhile, ProtectMyPrivacy (see Section 7.3.2) was another notable approach to dynamic analysis for iOS, published in 2013 (Agarwal and Hall, 2013). The authors of this tool developed an app for the Cydia store on jailbroken iPhones that monitored any attempted data access to sensitive information on the phone and blocked access as long as users had not given permission for this data processing.

Given the vastly increased complexity of recent versions of both ecosystems and the great difficulty in jailbreaking the latest iOS devices, neither approach has been pursued much in more recent research. Instead, many researchers have shifted to network traffic analysis to obtain insights into the real world practices of mobile apps. These approaches record apps' network traffic by directing it through software controlled by the researchers. For example, some researchers make their laptops act as an artificial WiFi hotspot to which they connect a mobile phone for testing. Other researchers have been using the virtual private network (VPN) or proxy functionality provided by Android and iOS (Ren et al, 2016; Shuba et al, 2018; Kollnig and Shadbolt, 2022).

One of the earliest approaches leveraging this approach was ReCon, dating back to 2016. These authors developed a VPN server capable of intercepting and reading the network traffic from Android, iOS, and Windows Phone. This interception relied on installing a self-signed certificate on the mobile phones so that the researchers could inspect even HTTPS-encrypted connections (man-in-the-middle attack). The server was running outside the phone, bringing a risk of data breaches. After all, the researchers could see all the transmitted data in clear text.

More modern approaches on Android have shifted to on-device VPNs rather than an external server. AntMonitor, released in 2015, is one of the most famous such tools (Le et al, 2015). It was an Android app that ran a VPN on the local Android through which other apps' network traffic was routed so that it could be inspected. The app even enabled users to check network traffic for sensitive information (like phone numbers and other identifiers) and replace any such occurrences with fake information.

Sadly, in the same year as the release of AntMonitor, Google also rolled out Android 7, which imposed tight restrictions on self-signed certificates. Now, it was no longer possible for users to intercept the network traffic of other apps unless they modified the system software on the phone. At the time, Google motivated the change with security concerns. This, however, has the direct effect that it becomes much more challenging for academic researchers, authorities, and other relevant stakeholders to inspect apps' supposedly encrypted network traffic. Interestingly, Apple has not implemented similar restrictions on iOS. They still allow self-signed certificates, making analysing apps' network traffic on iOS relatively easy. Instead, they use sophisticated user interface (UI) design to discourage inexperienced users from accidentally installing self-signed certificates from untrusted authorities, such as criminals who want to steal login details from apps' network traffic.

In light of this, it seems that Google was instead motivated by something other than security concerns: the loss of access to data and advertising revenue on Android. This is because the same tool that can reduce the unexpected leakage of users' personal data may also restrict Google's access to valuable data for its advertising business. Further, detailed insights into apps' network traffic also allow for the building of sophisticated ad-blocking tools. These have been demonstrated by NoMoAds, which uses an AI-based approach to ad blocking (Shuba et al, 2018). While ad blocker apps exist for the blocking of ads in other Android apps, these are unavailable directly via the Google Play Store (as demonstrated by the Disconnect.me app in Chapter 3) and suffer from over- or under-blocking (since ad blockers get much fewer insights into network traffic: contacted IP addresses only).

The increased use of a practice called 'certificate pinning' by many apps further makes analysing network traffic difficult. However, recently, Apple and Google have actively discouraged app developers from using these approaches (although both companies use them in system-level communications in Android and iOS). On Android, given an '.apk' file, this can be worked around with the tool apk-mitm.

A VPN/proxy approach tends to be relatively easy to implement for academic studies. For Android, I am actively maintaining the TrackerControl app that allows easy insights into apps' network communications. Among other aspects, the app gives straightforward access to the domains contacted by apps, the purposes of these domains, the companies that these domains belong to, and the country where these companies are based. Due to Android's restrictions, the app, however, gives no insights into the types of data that are being shared by apps. However, for an initial analysis of apps' data practices, the TrackerControl app can be helpful. A screenshot from the app is shown in Figure 5.2.

If one attempts to go more in-depth on either Android or iOS and analyse the contents of network traffic, then HTTP Toolkit provides an easy-to-use tool to get started. The basic version of this tool is provided for free and with extensive guidance and support from its creator, Tim Perry. The main limitation of the tool is also its greatest advantage: it's mainly a front-end-based system that cannot easily be automated in case one wants to test larger numbers of apps. Charles Proxy is another similar tool that is worth consideration.

Mitmproxy is usually the way to go to scale network traffic analysis across a larger number of apps. It is compatible with Android and iOS and is what I used for most of my research. However, this tool requires more technical configuration and expertise, which is beyond the scope of this book.

When choosing a device for app analysis, focusing on Android phones developed by Google (for example, the Nexus or Pixel line) is usually worthwhile. These phones run an unmodified 'stock' version of Android (and give insights that should generalise across other Android manufacturers), have few pre-installed apps that might affect analysis results, and allow bootloader unlocking. The latter is particularly important to install self-signed certificates and inspect the contents of apps' network traffic.

On iOS, older versions of iPhones or iPads are usually recommended because they allow the jailbreaking of the device and deeper analysis. At the time of writing, the only devices that run the latest iOS version and can be jailbroken are the entry-level iPads 2017, 2018, and 2019. They all use a central processing unit (CPU) that is vulnerable to the checkm8 exploit in the iPhone bootrom. Apple cannot change this bootrom through software updates because it is stored in read-only device memory.

While it is theoretically also possible to run apps in an emulator (instead of a real device), this approach tends to produce low-quality results. This

Figure 5.2: TrackerControl for Android, allowing simple static and dynamic analysis of Android apps

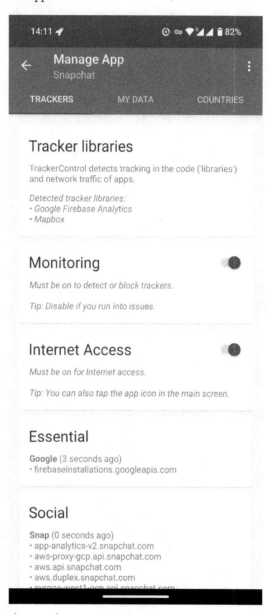

Source: https://trackercontrol.org

would be expected, given that emulators constitute a highly artificial, rather than a real world, environment.

5.2.2 Static analysis for insights at scale

Static analysis is a commonly used alternative to dynamic analysis. This approach tries to understand an app's behaviour without running it on a real device. As a result, this approach can scale more easily across large numbers of apps, but can sometimes struggle to give reliable evidence because apps are never run. This matters if, for example, one is interested in making complaints to a relevant public authority (or one is the public authority and seeks to hold apps' practices to account).

Flow analysis is one of the primary means of static analysis in the technical literature. By creating a control-flow graph (CFG) of an app of interest (that indicates all the possible paths that apps can take during execution on a real device), one can check whether apps may ever access and leak sensitive data. Given the high complexity of mobile apps (which regularly include the loading of additional code from remote sources), control flow analysis (CFA) is rarely complete and is thus prone to under-reporting. It is also prone to over-reporting if flows identified within an app are never actually executed on real devices. In other words, CFA gives an incomplete and hypothetical model of apps' real world behaviour.

A particularly innovative approach for CFA on iOS, called PiOS, was developed in 2011 (Egele et al, 2011). These authors behind PiOS overcame the challenges related to Apple's Objective-C programming language on iOS and reconstructed apps' CFGs to analyse sensitive data access. They found that, at that time, more than half of the apps could transmit the unique device ID of the device, enabling data brokers to create detailed user profiles. This practice was usually linked to apps using third-party advertising and analytics libraries, which were present in over half the studied apps. Interestingly, Egele et al (2011) found that apps from the alternative Cydia store had no worse behaviour in terms of access to sensitive data than apps from Apple's official App Store.

The CFA is computationally highly intensive and requires relatively sophisticated IT skills to analyse the resulting CFGs. Further, researchers, with their limited resources, struggle to keep up with the rapid pace of change and updates pushed by Apple and Google in their respective ecosystems. For example, PiOS is only compatible with Objective-C. However, today most new iOS apps are developed with Apple's new Swift programming language, for which no similar work exists.

In light of this, recent work has shifted to less sophisticated app analysis approaches. These give fewer insights into apps' behaviour, but are much quicker and simpler to run. The first impressive example of such an approach was the PlayDrone project (Viennot et al, 2014) by Nicolas Viennot, Edward Garcia, and Jason Nieh from Columbia University, published in 2016. They downloaded and analysed more than 1 million Android apps for the first time in an academic study. Analysing these apps, the authors found widespread security issues, including forgotten server keys inside the apps' code. Rather than conduct an end-to-end CFA, they used reverse engineering (which obtains readable programming code from the low-level CPU instructions in the app binary in the app package) to look for suspicious patterns in the studied apps.

Follow-up work from my Oxford research group from 2018 used a similar approach to study 1 million apps, but focused on data protection and privacy problems on Google Play (Binns et al, 2018). This study was motivated by the GDPR coming into force in May of the same year. These authors found that 90 per cent of apps could share data with Google and 40 per cent with Facebook. These findings were highly unexpected at the time and made it to the front page of the *Financial Times*. In a rare move, Google even issued a public response to the findings, casting doubt over the methodology used. This methodology did not rely heavily on reverse engineering but solely checked app packages for mentions of known tracking domains. If an app contained a reference, for example, 'analytics.google.com', then this app would be flagged as theoretically able to share data with Google. Because the work relied on static analysis, this would, however, not be definitive evidence of that necessarily happening in practice.

The most recent work on static analysis of apps does not rely on reverse engineering anymore, is incredibly fast to run, and is freely and easily available to anyone online through the Exodus Privacy project.[4] Interested individuals only have to enter the name of the app they are interested in on the Exodus Privacy website. After some waiting, the website shows which companies' apps can communicate with and what permissions apps can request. An API even exists, to which researchers can request access and analyse apps at a great scale. For iOS, a service exists[5] that applies a methodology similar to my TrackerControl app for Android (see Section 5.2.1) to iOS, but in a static way. A screenshot from my tool is shown in Figure 5.3.

A similar tool, which focuses on automated dynamic and static analysis and is not limited to privacy issues, is the Mobile Security Framework (MobSF).[6] This tool is highly comprehensive and relatively easy to use. A complete overview of this tool is, however, beyond the scope of this book.

5.2.3 Privacy policy and label analysis for additional insights

In some recent work, researchers have increasingly been interested in checking apps' behaviour as observed from dynamic and static analysis against

Figure 5.3: Exodus Privacy, but for iOS

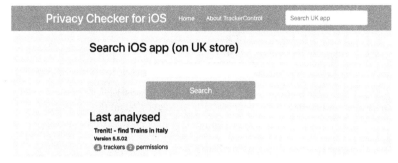

Source: https://ios.trackercontrol.org

the data practices that they disclose in their privacy policy or privacy nutrition label. Other researchers focus on policies or labels. Methodologically, these approaches build on recent advances in natural language processing (NLP), impressively demonstrated by software such as ChatGPT.

In 2018, Hamza Harkous and his colleagues at the École Polytechnique Fédérale de Lausanne (EPFL) built a tool called Polisis for the automated detection of privacy practices in privacy policies (Harkous et al, 2018). These authors were highly creative in making their technical methodology available and providing: (1) a chatbot in which individuals can ask questions about a given privacy policy; (2) a dedicated website and browser extension that visualises all the outcomes from their analysis of any given privacy policy; and (3) an API for other researchers to access the analysis results. The latter has been beneficial for many follow-up studies.

Zimmeck et al (2019) combined static and policy analysis to analyse more than 1 million Android apps. Their work identified typical inconsistencies and discrepancies between the data practices described in apps' privacy policies and those performed by apps. Similarly, Okoyomon et al (2019) found, by analysing keywords in privacy policies, widespread compliance issues of children's apps regarding the Children's Online Privacy Protection Act (COPPA), the US privacy law to protect children's privacy. These authors found widespread discrepancies between disclosed app behaviour and what was observed in apps' network traffic. The potential of policy analysis is constrained by the limitations of the methods used to analyse policies, such as NLP's limited analytical and logical reasoning abilities, compounded by the incompleteness and ambiguity inherent in many privacy policies (Reidenberg et al, 2016).

Studies on privacy labels have noticed a similar discrepancy between apps' disclosed and actual data practices (Kollnig et al, 2022). Indeed, the privacy labels on the App Store are self-disclosed by app developers and not regularly checked by Apple. Meanwhile, if apps show in-app disclosures, Google allows app publishers not to disclose certain data practices in the privacy labels. As a result, the Apple and Google store labels are bound to be incomplete, if not misleading, for consumers.

In sum, neither the privacy labels nor the privacy policies currently give sufficient insights into apps' data practices. Although by being public facing on the app stores, they might seem like an accessible source of valuable information for researchers, they should only ever be analysed with great care.

5.2.4 Obstacles to research due to Apple and Google's decisions

As discussed in Section 4.2, the GDPR places stringent obligations on the organisations that control the processing of personal data. This could, to an extent, also extend to the practices of Apple and Google insofar as their explicit decisions inhibit transparency of data practices in mobile apps. Some of my research found that there is reason to believe that a wide variety of such measures are taken by Apple and Google, which inhibit researchers' ability to hold apps' data practices to account and, as a result, have negative effects on app privacy in general (Kollnig and Shadbolt, 2023).

To this end, I reviewed over 100 academic papers and identified many deliberate techniques employed by Apple and Google to make their app ecosystems less transparent and accountable. For example, neither Apple nor Google currently provides public APIs for the study of apps on the app stores. Such APIs would allow researchers to obtain information about apps on the app stores in a structured manner, including details about apps' ranking and popularity, pricing and monetisation, and privacy properties. Meanwhile, Apple does provide this information to advertisers through its affiliate marketing programme. Thus, it would be straightforward for Apple to extend data access. In the interim, two options remain for researchers: (1) either spend a significant amount of time to develop data collection approaches for their specific needs (as explained in this chapter); or (2) contract the services of specialised third-party companies, such as 42matters that charge researchers tens of thousands of euros for data access, as discussed earlier in this chapter. Especially for researchers who seek to study historical trends in app stores or have limited technical expertise, contracting a third party would remain the only option. Fortunately, with the DSA, a third approach emerges: using its research data access rules. The following section will provide more details on this.

Another example stems from Android and its de facto ban on self-signed certificates. As discussed earlier in this chapter, these certificates used to be instrumental for analysing apps' network traffic, like AntMonitor. Without such certificates, researchers can only study what domains are contacted by apps, but none of the actual data that is being exchanged. It is possible to turn off these protections on some Android phones by modifying the underlying operating system; this requires time and effort. Many popular apps even stop working when they detect a modified operating system, a chicken-and-egg problem. The alleged reason for this ban was Google's concerns about end user security. However, self-signed certificates also allow the development of sophisticated ad blockers for mobile apps. Wide adoption of such technology would hurt Google's core business model in mobile ads. Thus, the company decided to eliminate this threat, similar to how they did with Disconnect.me (see Section 3.4). On iOS, these restrictions do not exist, which underlines that Apple and Google have a choice in choosing to opt for this ban.

A last example stems from the Apple App Store. The download of iOS apps can be accomplished in a relatively straightforward manner with the iTunes software or IPAtool; however, every app downloaded from the App Store is encrypted with Apple's FairPlay Digital Rights Management (DRM). The decryption is necessary for the in-depth study of iOS apps and is relatively straightforward. It could, however, also violate international copyright law, which prohibits the circumvention of DRM. As a result, the decryption of iOS apps could, theoretically, result in criminal charges, especially if performed for tens of thousands of apps, a typical number of apps for research studies. The encryption is applied to all iOS apps, even free ones.

It is important to note that copyright law was not designed to prevent researchers from doing their jobs, and they are most likely allowed to engage in the decryption of iOS apps in most jurisdictions. Indeed, many jurisdictions have explicit exemptions for specific types of research. For example, vulnerability research is exempt from the restrictions in the US. However, it is not always clear how narrow the definition of 'vulnerability research' is and if, for example, my research on app privacy and compliance would fall under the existing exemptions. While probably fine, a risk remains for researchers that needs to be carefully considered, depending on the specific jurisdiction. If this risk is deemed too high, alternative approaches, like those developed in my research, should be considered.

However, the case *United States v. Elcom Ltd* underlines the potential risks researchers open themselves up to if they operate in the grey areas of copyright law. In this case, Dmitry Sklyarov visited the US to give a talk on the shortcomings of Adobe's copyright protections in eBooks. Sklyarov was arrested for 2 weeks and then released on bail. He was cleared of all charges a few months later and could only then leave the US again for his home in Russia. The case underlines the risk that researchers potentially open themselves up to by operating within grey areas of copyright law. The fact that Apple continues to apply copyright protection to all apps downloaded from the Apple App Store is unacceptable from the perspective of many in the research community.

Meanwhile, Android pursues a more nuanced strategy. Here, paid apps are also encrypted, as a measure against privacy, but not free apps. In response, much of my past research has been dedicated to studying Apple apps without the need for decryption, with the aim of developing methods that do not pose risks to researchers.

The primary reason for using encryption is to protect app publishers against piracy, that is, lost revenue from illegal app copies. For the longest time, paid apps on Android have been relatively uncommon because it's always been easy to circumvent Google's restrictions and sideload pirated apps. However, on iOS, piracy also remains rampant, and sideloading is common, especially in the Chinese market. This makes it somewhat absurd to apply these protections in the first place and makes one wonder whether Apple intentionally uses copyright law against researchers to make independent scrutiny harder, especially since the encryption is also applied to free apps.

The practices mentioned in this section could pose problems for Apple and Google under the DSA. After all, the law singles out challenges to EU citizens' data protection and privacy rights as potential systemic risks. If these challenges are systemic, Apple and Google must implement adequate remedies. Given that privacy problems in apps are well-documented, there is good reason to believe that Apple and Google will need to provide researchers adequate access to data relating to app privacy if these researchers request such data. Chapter 11 will give more specific recommendations on how to accomplish this.

5.3 Using the DSA for platform data access

As discussed in Section 4.3.3, Article 40 of the DSA is supposed to give researchers access to platforms' data so that they can analyse systemic risks facilitated by those platforms. The information researchers can request includes public and non-public information, under Article 40(12) and Article 40(4) of the DSA, respectively.

At the time of writing, access to non-public data is not possible. The European Commission must first develop a so-called Delegated Act, outlining the exact conditions and procedures for platform data access. This is expected for 2025, after which the national authorities must implement the Delegated Act.

Meanwhile, researchers already have access to public platform data. However, it is highly restricted, as I have found. In the case of Apple and Google, the researcher must first fill out a lengthy questionnaire to request platform data. In the questionnaire, among other things, it must be explained what one wishes to study, how this relates to systemic risks facilitated by the platform, what (public) data is needed for this study, and where the research funding comes from. The exact requirements are spelled out in Article 40.

In practice, I found that Google goes beyond what is legally required, which can be discouraging for some researchers, costs more time, and might be illegal. My first request to Google was rejected once due to unexplained reasons, which was further discouraging. A copy of the application should be saved before submission because the entered details cannot be accessed anymore after submission, which I hadn't. Meanwhile, Apple sifted through all my public information and tried to find a conflict of interest on my part due to commercial interests, of which I don't have any and of which they also didn't find any.

Once the request is granted, the data that was applied for can be accessed. In my case, I tried to apply for all the data shown on the front ends of app stores, as well as the app packages, which should cover most of the publicly available data of the app stores. Apple was most helpful in providing that data. They assembled the data for me, so I just needed to download it via a link they provided. However, they didn't provide instructions on how to work with that data and used a difficult-to-understand data format. Working with this data, therefore, takes time and requires strong IT skills. This will probably be addressed as more researchers work with the data. Moving forward, this data promises to provide better insights into the App Store, including a better grasp of what apps exist on the store. App exploration, as discussed in Section 5.1.2, is then no longer necessary.

Sadly, Apple rejected my request for a copy of the apps on the App Store because they held that they weren't public information in the meaning of the law. Although this is a surprising interpretation (apps don't seem non-public), and I disagree, it's difficult to challenge this claim as a researcher; this would usually lie with the responsible authority that I reached out to immediately for clarification. However, they claimed that they couldn't do anything until the European Commission had adopted the Delegated Act mentioned earlier in this section.

Meanwhile, Google solely provided a short, eight-page document, which was supposed to give instructions for data access but didn't contain any helpful information. Rather than provide data to researchers directly, they hold that their job is done by permitting researchers to use scripts, such as those described earlier in this chapter. In addition, they also requested my permanent public IP address, which I don't have, so that they wouldn't block me accidentally from downloading said data via that IP address.

Overall, the DSA, so far, provides limited help in accessing platform data. Apple provides some data, and Google provides none at all.

5.4 A long way to go for platform data access

Over the past decades, a wealth of approaches have emerged to study apps. They each come with their limitations. Static analysis approaches like

Exodus Privacy provide insights into tracker libraries integrated into apps. However, they may miss certain libraries if they are not known to Exodus or if developers use custom integration methods. Static analysis may also falsely detect tracking when code relating to tracking is present in an app but never used when the app is run on a real phone.

Better evidence can be generated with dynamic analysis approaches, but these can be more challenging to use. They may also give incomplete analysis results if not all functionality within an app is tested when running the app. There are usually also some gaps in the analysis due to the apps' use of countermeasures against independent analysis, such as code obfuscation or custom encryption of data flows. Some dynamic analysis tools like TrackerControl use statistical methods to determine what domain name belongs to an IP address and may give false results. TrackerControl is currently only meant as a first line of analysis. More sophisticated approaches are necessary for analysing network traffic, at best, those that use man-in-the-middle approaches and obtain the domain name directly from (unencrypted) HTTP requests.

Legal approaches, particularly those under the DSA, promise to address current challenges when studying mobile apps. However, they are held back by immaturity and platforms' known unwillingness to cooperate with researchers, even when it comes to human rights matters. For example, the DSA already provides access to publicly accessible app store information. Still, neither Apple nor Google currently provides access to app packages, which are key to studying apps' practices. The DSA's rules on access to non-public research data and platform data access laws in other countries, such as the UK, might finally help move the needle. In the meantime, my research could, once again, be the only study into iOS app privacy in about a decade.

PART II

Risks

6

App Monetisation and Moderation

The two companies, Apple and Google, govern their respective ecosystems with different strategies that directly impact the monetisation models of app developers. These strategies, in turn, limit the extent to which individuals can exert various fundamental rights and freedoms. This chapter will focus on the impact of the gatekeepers' governance strategies on individuals' rights to freedom of business and freedom of speech. Figure 6.1 compares these different revenue models visually.

Apple has traditionally derived most of its revenue from mobile device sales, which make up 75 per cent of its total revenue in 2024. Driven by a wish to control the whole iPhone/iPad supply chain, the company does not licence iOS to other device manufacturers, also known as OEMs. Apple devices cater to the premium sector of loyal, high-paying customers who promise higher margins than the budget sector. This makes tight control of the supply chain ever more critical for Apple to be able to fulfil high consumer expectations.

Meanwhile, Google's strategy is geared towards maximum adoption of its Android ecosystem (Holzer and Ondrus, 2011). To this end, Google makes most of Android's code available as open source. The exception from this open source strategy is the code of the standard Google apps, including the Google Play Store and Play Services, which comprise an essential part of the Android ecosystem (see Chapter 2 and the US lawsuit in Section 4.4.2). The OEMs may licence these additional services from Google for a fee and further contractual obligations (The Verge, 2018). Nowadays, many Android apps do not work unless the device comes with proprietary services, such as the Google Play Services. In this sense, Google has become more like Apple over the years, because it gained a robust market share and drove out competitors, such as Nokia, Microsoft, RIM, Palm, and Mozilla, each of which once tried to develop their competing smartphone operating systems (Symbian, Windows Phone, Blackberry OS, webOS, and Firefox OS).

Google chooses a strategy of maximum adoption since most of its revenue in the mobile app ecosystem does not derive from device sales

Figure 6.1: Revenue streams of Apple and Google compared

Apple	Google
Device sales	**Advertising**
~75% of 2024 revenue	**~76% of 2024 revenue**
Focus on premium hardware (iPhone/iPad), sales driven most revenue	Most revenue from ads (Search, YouTube, Network), powered by user data
Services	**Non-advertising revenue**
~25% of 2024 revenue	**~24% of 2024 revenue**
Significant revenue from various services, including:	Includes Google Cloud, hardware, and other services like:
App Store (commissions), advertising (search ads), licensing (e.g. Google search deal), iCloud+ and Apple Music	Google Play Store (commissions), Licensing fees (OEMs), subscriptions (e.g. YouTube Premium), and hardware sales (Pixel, Nest, Fitbit)

Source: Alphabet (2024) and Apple (2024c)

or other fees but rather from mobile advertising. In 2024, Alphabet, Google's parent company, generated $265 billion (76 per cent) of its revenue from advertising, with more than half of that generated on mobile devices. Google's mobile advertising business is so lucrative because its privileged position in the Android ecosystem gives it better data access than most of its competitors, which, in turn, is a key ingredient when deriving revenue from personalised advertising. As a rule of thumb, more users translate into more eyeballs and data and, by extension, more ad revenue. The link between monetisation in mobile apps and the large-scale collection of sensitive data has caused concerns about the resulting impacts on individuals' fundamental rights and freedoms, including the rights to data protection and privacy rights (Chen et al, 2016; Vines et al, 2017; Binns et al, 2018; Reardon et al, 2019). This aspect will be further explored in Chapter 7.

In terms of revenue streams, both platforms take a share of up to 30 per cent of all direct revenues created from app sales and in-app purchases (IAPs), but differ otherwise. Additionally, app developers face restrictions over the payment methods, outside of the ones provided by Apple and Google, that they can use to sell services to their users. Laws, such as the DMA, are addressing this, but their implications have been limited so far.

6.1 Monetisation in apps and loss of property

In the app ecosystem, there are two primary ways of monetisation: (1) ad-based models; and (2) paid-for models (Appel et al, 2020). In Category 2, further subcategories exist, particularly paid apps, IAPs, and subscriptions. Which one of these models is used largely depends on whether you use Android or iOS. Since iOS tends to cater to, on average, wealthier individuals, paid-for models are more common here. They also align better with Apple's business model in selling physical devices.

In 2020, about 15.4 per cent of apps on the UK Google Play and 22.5 per cent of iOS apps offered IAPs; this makes IAPs 1.5 times more common on iOS than on Google Play (Kollnig et al, 2022a). The size of the market for IAPs has been growing rapidly over time. For example, in the US, $30.4 billion was spent on IAPs in 2020 and $37.4 billion in 2021; these figures are projected to increase vastly over the years to come (eMarketer, 2022). Meanwhile, the importance of paid apps has declined. About 10 per cent of apps were paid on the App Store in 2019; this figure has dropped to about 5 per cent (Statista, 2023b). Meanwhile, paid apps have always been an exception on the Google Play Store, making up about 3 per cent of all available apps (Statista, 2023a). From the perspective of app developers, IAPs offer steadier and reliable revenue streams than one-off app purchases.

One might believe that apps with IAPs come with less advertising. However, 95 per cent of apps with IAPs on Android could also access the Advertising Identifier, which is linked to advertising, and 78.4 per cent of apps on iOS (Kollnig et al, 2022a). This suggests that IAPs are usually used in conjunction with ads and may indeed be an incentive for end users to purchase an ad-free version of an app through an IAP. This, however, might create an incentive for app developers to bombard users increasingly with many low-quality ads to turn them into paying customers rather than making ad revenue (which might also be higher for ads that, at first sight, look like they are low-quality but may engage in excessive data sharing or advertise for shady products, such as other apps with this monetisation strategy). As for whether paid apps come with less advertising, this seems to be true. However, they do not necessarily come with better privacy properties. Many paid apps collect and share user data just as extensively as their free equivalents (Han et al, 2020; Laperdrix et al, 2022).

The emphasis on specific business models is intentional. Google has traditionally allowed sideloading on Android and implements only minimal restrictions against piracy, that is, the illicit copying and distribution of paid apps. This makes it simple for Android users to obtain and install free copies of paid apps. Ironically, all one needs to do is turn to Google Search and follow the steps described there. Therefore, Google heavily discourages paid apps and encourages ad-driven business models. This helps Google in multiple ways, by manifesting its dominance in the ad sector (for example, by making the use of Google Ads simple in apps and encouraging spill-over effects to websites) and, in turn, gaining access to even more personal data to improve its ad targeting.

The iOS ecosystem is more locked down, which makes piracy more difficult. Locking down iOS ensures that Apple receives its 'app store tax' of 30 per cent commission and prevents other apps from working around it.

However, there have been reports from app developers that they face similar threats from illicit copying (Li et al, 2020). This is somewhat surprising, given that Apple has long publicly prided itself on stringent restrictions on sideloading that are meant to keep the app stores safe for app users and developers. What Apple rarely communicates is that they have long-established, reliable channels for sideloading, even before the DMA (see Section 4.3.2).

From the perspective of users, the shift away from paid apps is part of wider societal movements away from ownership. Before the smartphone era, individuals would buy a copy of software, books or videos; this practice is now much more uncommon. Smartphones have contributed to the loss of our sense of property, and instead merely issue software licences. These licences are often temporary, as in the case of subscription models that give end users a limited right to use an app-based service and can be revoked at any time. Indeed, Google and Apple's policies explicitly state that they may remove downloaded apps from users' phones at any time. Frequent app updates, faster internet speeds, and faster software development cycles further fuel this loss of property and sense of ownership. These updates are often incompatible with each other, so frequent updating (and constant renewal of subscriptions/licences) becomes necessary. Apple and Google's lack of action against piracy further contributes to this loss of ownership, discouraging paid apps. This has direct negative consequences for data use and attention since the alternatives to paid apps, IAPs, and in-app ads rely on increasing user interaction with the app. This will be further discussed in the next section.

6.2 App store tax and implications for prices

One might think that there is no problem with having Google and Apple competing in the smartphone ecosystem. After all, in classical economic theory, they would try to undercut each other in prices and eventually charge consumers only as much as is required to run their services. However, there are a few doubts about this.

First, modern economic theory, particularly behavioural economics, holds that key assumptions behind classical economic theory are flawed. For example, consumers may choose not to switch from Android to iOS (or vice versa) because of convenience; some users may choose an iOS device not because it's better than all Android counterparts but because they've always had one. This would not be reflected in classical economic theory, which assumes that individuals always act rationally in their economic decision making and only consider the costs incurred in choosing between Android and iOS.

Second, related to the previous point, the assumption that the market around smartphone operating systems would be perfect is flawed. For example, high switching costs currently exist between Android and iOS. Purchases cannot be transferred. iMessages only exist on iOS. Phone backups are incompatible between Android and iOS (including WhatsApp and Signal backups), and many other aspects.

Third, as discussed previously, iOS and Android cater to different segments of consumers. iOS is only available on iPhones, which are unaffordable for some individuals due to their higher prices (Competition and Markets Authority, 2022b).

A symptom of a lack of competition in the ecosystem is that the maximum fee (30 per cent of app revenues) charged by Apple and Google has not changed since their app stores were introduced (Competition and Markets Authority, 2022b). These companies may convincingly argue that it was necessary to build the underlying systems in the early days of smartphones. However, this argument is hardly convincing anymore, more than a decade after both app stores were introduced and following substantial consolidation in the market.

The app store fees are similar to those charged by Visa and Mastercard on credit and debit card transactions. In the UK, the two companies have a combined market share of 99 per cent and, therefore, constitute a duopoly in the market for payment cards. Despite this, the typical fees are much lower, from 0.20 per cent to 0.30 per cent. This is because the EU Regulation 2015/751 caps them for domestic transactions in Europe (including the UK) at this level.

The app store tax has led to several ongoing disputes, most notably between Apple and Epic Games, the developer of the popular game Fortnite. In August 2020, Epic Games introduced a direct payment system within the Fortnite app for iOS that bypassed the IAP system and Apple's 30 per cent commission on all transactions. In response, Apple removed Fortnite from the App Store, which barred users from downloading or updating the app on iOS devices.

Epic Games filed a lawsuit against Apple, arguing that removing Fortnite from the App Store violated US antitrust laws and that the 30 per cent commission on IAPs is excessive and due to Apple's abuse of market dominance. Apple defended its actions, stating that removing Fortnite resulted from violating the App Store guidelines and that the commission was necessary to cover the costs of running the store. After appeals up to the US Supreme Court, the courts determined that Apple had not violated US antitrust laws but California consumer protection law. Apple must now allow developers to link to alternative payment methods inside iOS apps. In response to these concerns, other jurisdictions, such as the EU, the

Netherlands, and South Korea, have also enacted new regulations that force Apple and Google to revise their payment structure.

Another symptom of a lack of competition is that Google is the most widely used search engine in the West, on both mobile and desktop devices. It is even the default engine on iOS. This is partly because Google has paid Apple tens of billions of dollars to remain the default setting in the Safari browser, the default on Apple devices. These payments amount to a third of Google's total advertising revenue on Apple devices and underline how closely Apple's revenues are tied to Google's advertising and invasive data collection (BBC, 2023).

The net result of this lack of competition in the app ecosystem is likely unnecessarily high prices for consumers. For example, every paid app or IAP acquired through the app stores is significantly more expensive than it may need to be due to the commission that Apple and Google take. Further, Google has a de facto monopoly over advertising in search engines (in addition to other markets). According to StatCounter, Google holds over 90 per cent of the market share in online search engines. As a result, the company can charge higher prices than would be necessary in a competitive market environment. The result of the previous market prices for search ads is that any product promoted through Google Ads becomes more expensive than it should be in a perfect market. In addition to higher prices, a lack of sufficient competition is often argued to lead to reduced product quality as well.

6.3 Content moderation and freedom of speech

To support the success of their business strategies (in ads and device sales), Google and Apple tightly control what practices are permitted on the official app stores. Traditionally, Google's approach to content moderation on the app store has been more lenient than that of Apple, which has a much stricter set of guidelines (for example, regarding app design or data protection). Apple relies more on manual app reviews based on review policies that are not always clear or consistent (Gilen and Shilton, 2018).

The content moderation of Apple and Google has the effect that these platforms decide which business models are permissible and how other businesses should be run. For example, limited sexual content currently exists on the App Store because Steve Jobs had a strong aversion to such content. Famously, Jobs proclaimed that 'we believe we have a moral responsibility to keep porn off the iPhone. Folks who want porn can buy an ... Android phone.' (CNET, 2010) As a result of these policies, the apps from widely known news organisations were previously taken down from the app stores, including *Stern* (2009) and *Bild* (2010), two leading German newspapers. Mathias Müller von Blumencron, the editor of *Der Spiegel* (another German newspaper), noted that they 'can't adapt European magazines to the standards of Utah' (*The New York Times*, 2010).

Yoel Roth, the former Head of Security at Twitter, published a widely regarded opinion piece in *The New York Times* in November 2022 (*The New York Times, 2022*). He argued that Apple and Google 'may be the most significant check on unrestrained speech on the mainstream internet'. He explained that failure 'to adhere to Apple's and Google's guidelines would be catastrophic' for Twitter. While laws play a part in shaping these guidelines, he claimed that 'platform policies are shaped by the preferences of a small group of predominantly American tech executives'. Ultimately, he chose to resign from his post because he felt that under Elon Musk's leadership, Twitter would not be able to overcome the same hypocrisy between guiding free speech and unaccountable decisions by Musk.

On Google Play, the company bans ad and tracking blockers. According to Google's policies, this ban on ad blockers is based on the claim that such apps may 'interfere with ... other apps on the device' (Google, 2024). Based on this policy, Google banned the Disconnect.me privacy app twice, once in 2014 and once in 2015. This app, developed by a former Google employee and another software engineer, enabled end users to reduce apps' unwanted data sharing with third-party companies. The app was explicitly not targeted at ads, which are the core of Google's business model.

Interestingly, the DuckDuckGo browser released a similar tracking-blocking feature for all Android users in November 2022. Google has not yet banned this app from the Play Store, even though it conflicts with the same policy. This highlights that the review policies can be overly broad and are enforced arbitrarily. It also highlights that consumer expectations of privacy have significantly changed over the past few years, and concerns around the disproportionate power of large tech companies are now at the top of the agenda of regulatory authorities worldwide. As a result, Apple and Google are more restricted in content moderation than they used to be.

Another case stems from the attack on the US Capitol on 6 January 2021, which the then-President Trump partly incited. In the aftermath, it was alleged that the right-wing social media app Parler was used to help coordinate the riots. The app advertises itself as 'Speak Freely' and is used to implement minimal content moderation.

In response to the Capitol attack, Apple and Google removed the Parler app from their app stores a few days later. Additionally, Amazon ended the hosting of Parler's web services. A revised app, with tightened content restrictions, was published on the App Store on 17 May 2021 and, almost 1.5 years later, on Google Play on 2 September 2022.

While the Parler case is arguably a positive example to support the healthy flourishing of democracies, the mentioned cases highlight the influence that decisions by Apple and Google have on the freedom of speech and the freedom to conduct business. They also underline a one-size-fits-all approach, where the standards of American executives with business interests in China are exported around the globe.

The last case stems from the email app 'Hey', a premium email service that costs $99 per year. Their services, again and again, have been rejected by Apple on the App Store because a login is necessary to use an account. Apple's rationale behind this is relatively straightforward: Hey must be purchased by users on its website, resulting in Apple not receiving its 30 per cent share of Hey's revenue. However, Hey successfully went public with Apple's repeated rejections, leading to bad PR in an environment where Apple is already under pressure over having too much power in the app economy. Eventually, Apple changed its App Store rules in response to the media response, now including a carve-out from the 30 per cent commission for email apps like Hey (Hey, 2024).

6.4 Apple's dependence on China

'Apple and China ... grew together and so this has been a symbiotic kind of relationship,' said Apple CEO Tim Cook in 2023 at the China Development Forum, the Chinese version of Davos (*Financial Times*, 2023b). Apple and China, as much of the modern US economy, have developed a deep relationship over the past two decades, ever since China joined the World Trade Organisation (WTO) in 2002.

To fulfil the global demand for Apple products, the company had to build vast, robust, and efficient manufacturing capabilities. The Chinese economy, with its large, skilled workforce and relatively flexible interpretation of applicable laws as they pertain to economic growth, was fundamental to Apple's success.

Driven by Steve Jobs' pursuit of perfection in their products, Apple established tightly controlled and highly efficient supply chains. The company remains the most profitable smartphone company; many of its competitors, including HTC, Ericsson, Nokia, and Blackberry, have left the smartphone business over fierce competition, limited revenues, and monopolisation of market access.

During the COVID-19 pandemic and the Russian invasion of Ukraine, the world has been confronted with how vulnerable supply chains are that rely on only one country. For example, in April 2022, Apple Chief Finance Officer (CFO) Luca Maestri warned of declines in Apple sales of up to $8 billion due to supply chain constraints related to COVID-19 lockdowns in China (CNBC, 2022). The ongoing conflict between the US and China over Taiwan, home to the Taiwan Semiconductor Manufacturing Company (TSMC), further adds to uncertainty in Apple's supply chain. TSMC is

Apple's primary producer of computing chips for its entire product line, including iPhones, iPads, Macs, and Apple Watches.

In the same way Europe had to shift its energy supplies away from Russia, Apple is now trying to move away from China. However, no single country can currently provide a similarly massive, educated, and cheap workforce as China. There are some attempts by Apple to shift to Vietnam and India; however, these efforts are in their infancy and rely significantly on parts being manufactured in China (*Financial Times*, 2023a; 2023c). In response to the latest batch of US tariffs against China, from 2026, Apple wants to assemble most iPhones for the US market in India (Reuters, 2025). However, this will hardly change the fact that much of the underlying electronics for Apple products will still be made in China. It is simply infeasible to quickly redirect decades of Apple's investment in Chinese infrastructure elsewhere. Matching the unique workforce of China will be even harder.

Meanwhile, the Chinese market is also one of Apple's largest markets. Its products are beloved by Chinese citizens. An Apple device is, more so than in many Western countries with higher average incomes, a symbol of status and wealth. Apple is the only major Western tech company that operates in China. Google left China in 2010 over censorship concerns and backlash from its employees. Microsoft shut down LinkedIn over similar concerns in China in 2021. Amazon China has never gained traction and has dramatically scaled down since 2019. Facebook and Twitter never entered the market and are unavailable in China.

Operating in China requires Apple to navigate the country's strict set of internal rules. Personal data is stored on Chinese servers, unlike Apple's operations in other parts of the world. Apps, particularly VPNs, news, and messaging apps, must be made unavailable when requested by the authorities. For example, in April 2024, it was reported that the Cyberspace Administration of China ordered Apple to remove popular Western messaging apps, including WhatsApp, Signal, and Telegram, from its App Store (Reuters, 2024a). While they hadn't been operational in China before, they were still available for download and use outside of China, or with a VPN. This underlines that a global set of norms and values simply does not exist, being in stark conflict with Apple's philosophy that embraces simplicity and a one-size-fits-all approach. This is discussed further in Chapter 8.

Hardly any company is so tightly integrated between the US and China. This forces Apple to engage continuously in difficult balancing acts between two nations that have become increasingly hostile to each other. Should Sino–American relations worsen, the company may need to shift further away from China. It may need to pull out completely, as it did with Russia following its invasion of Ukraine. The employees of Chinese authorities have already been ordered not to use Apple devices anymore, a blow to

Apple's China business, and a nod to the loss of confidence in US products in China (Bloomberg, 2023).

6.5 Much focus on markets in current regulation

The regulatory focus on app stores so far tends to focus on the fees charged on the app stores and how the gatekeepers might abuse their dominance for their good, as highlighted by the Epic Games case. This is understandable, given that substantial financial interests are at play between providers of app stores and publishers of apps, both seeking financial gain. In response, the EU's DMA obliges Apple and Google to allow developers to use alternative payment methods under fair conditions.

Beyond these financial and market considerations, so far, there has been little debate over how decisions taken by Apple and Google translate into practices inside apps and how those have more widespread ramifications on how we live as societies. Other platform ecosystems, such as e-commerce or social media, attract much more scrutiny over concerns around self-preferencing, the spread of disinformation, and impacts on elections.

One might ask why we should care about app stores and what harm they cause. This chapter underlines that app stores affect monetisation strategies (including the incentives for collecting fine-grained data to support IAPs or advertising-driven business models), global supply chains (including Apple's reliance on China), and the protection of fundamental rights (including freedom of speech and to conduct business). The providers of the app stores have an incentive to make quality apps available and usually do not enforce complete bans on most kinds of apps. There have been some notable bans, including Parler and Disconnect.me; however, those haven't been widely used apps, or at least not yet. Parler has even been reinstated now that they have incorporated more stringent moderation policies. However, there's something to Yoel Roth's claim that there's one power that doesn't get talked about much on the internet, that of Apple and Google in the app economy. When apps are in their infancy and are removed or are subject to stringent rules, this has notable effects on the direction of innovation and business.

The following chapters will investigate these harms further, first by looking more deeply into concerns around privacy and data protection in apps in the next chapter.

(The Lack of) Data Protection, Privacy, and the Rule of Law

You may have heard of Apple's advertising campaign 'Privacy. That's iPhone.' However, does this claim hold up to reality? To date, Apple provides minimal empirical evidence despite aggressively touting iOS as the more privacy-preserving mobile operating system compared with Android.

In the aftermath of the EU's GDPR (which came into force in 2016; see Section 4.2), it has often been criticised that the number of 'consent' banners proliferated online. According to this law, consent must be a 'freely given, specific, informed and unambiguous' choice, a standard that is rarely met in practice. Driven by the high potential fines under the GDPR (up to 4per cent of a company's annual global turnover), an industry of Consent Management Platforms (CMPs) emerged in response to help software developers pretend that they fulfil their consent obligations. Figure 7.1 shows a common example where consent is far from 'free' but instead is hidden behind a submenu ('Manage Preferences'). Many CMP companies boast opt-in rates of up to 95 per cent (CookiePro, 2021; Didomi, 2021). It appears unlikely that such a high figure could be achieved consistently across apps and websites without any form of coercion or nudging of users into giving consent. There is a vast gap between the law on the books and the reality in software.

In practice, few individuals feel empowered and that they face 'free' and 'informed' choices; however, they are deeply frustrated over the sheer number of privacy choices, many of which are deceptive and ineffective. Indeed, the overwhelming majority of consent flows violate the GDPR, as found in my own and other research (Matte et al, 2019; Nouwens et al, 2020; Veale et al, 2022). Sadly, public authorities are not managing to keep up. Meanwhile, private enforcement is challenging because it is difficult to prove damage from privacy violations and claim compensation from offending companies.

Despite all this consent bullying, many individuals care deeply about their privacy, but are often just not given genuine choices. According to the Pew

Figure 7.1: An example of a commonly seen cookie banner

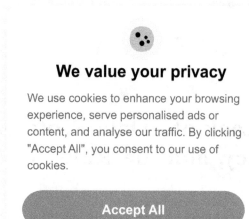

We value your privacy

We use cookies to enhance your browsing experience, serve personalised ads or content, and analyse our traffic. By clicking "Accept All", you consent to our use of cookies.

Accept All

Manage Preferences

Research Center, in 2019, almost two-thirds of US adults believed that their online behaviour was regularly tracked by companies (62 per cent) and the government (63 per cent) (Pew Research Center, 2019). About 80 per cent of surveyed adults felt like they had limited control over their data and held that the benefits of data collection commonly outweigh the risks.

Since privacy remains a key issue with mobile devices, this chapter analyses this issue in detail, particularly how the decisions by Google and Apple play a role. We will see that both companies, Apple and Google, have profited immensely from a relative lack of privacy protections in their respective ecosystems and that their deliberate erosion of privacy standards has, in turn, undermined individuals' norms and expectations of privacy over time.

7.1 What is privacy?

Privacy is a highly individual concept. One of the most widely accepted definitions stems from Helen Nissenbaum, who characterised privacy as 'contextual integrity' (Nissenbaum, 2004). This reflects that all individuals share information about themselves differently, depending on the context, to protect their privacy. For instance, many individuals would not share the same information with colleagues at work as they do with their loved ones. Similarly, members of the LGBTQ community in many countries still face negative consequences from sharing their sexual preferences openly and, therefore, need to be careful when sharing information.

In light of such challenges, privacy is essential for one's flourishing and the development of one's identity, both of which are fundamental aspects of human rights law. This is why privacy is an important societal norm and a legally protected right in many countries. Indeed, Article 12 of the United Nations (UN) Universal Declaration of Human Rights, which has about 200 signatories, states that, 'No one shall be subjected to arbitrary interference with his *privacy*, family, home or correspondence, nor to attacks upon his honour and reputation. Everyone has the right to the protection of the law against such interference or attacks.'

Admittedly, it can be difficult to translate the concept of privacy into software. The concept of privacy can be very individual and context-dependent. Because there is no clear translation into software, many conflicts and challenges emerge around privacy, as discussed in this chapter.

A closely related concept, also considered a fundamental right in many countries, is 'data protection'. This, in turn, is rooted in the idea of 'informational self-determination', first introduced by the 1983 landmark ruling of the German Federal Constitutional Court. The highest German court concluded that

> In the context of modern data processing, [human dignity, particularly the right to personal identity,] encompasses the protection of the individual against unlimited collection, storage, use and sharing of personal data. The fundamental right guarantees the authority conferred on the individual to, in principle, decide himself on the disclosure and use of their personal data. Limitations of this right to '*informational self-determination*' are only permissible if there is an overriding public interest. (First Senate of the Bundesverfassungsgericht, 1983)

In other words, informational self-determination means that an individual should have control over the data that relates to them. Such data is called 'personal data' in the GDPR. As such, informational self-determination is similar to the concept of property (where individuals own and can decide on physical goods), yet not quite the same. Like privacy, data protection is part of EU human rights law and protected under Article 8 of the EU Charter of Fundamental Rights. This is what the GDPR aims to protect. Rather than being a privacy law (as often claimed), it aims to protect all fundamental rights, and data protection in particular.

The exact difference between privacy and data protection has been debated much in the academic literature (Kokott and Sobotta, 2013; Lynskey, 2015). In a nutshell, they have slightly different scopes and meanings, which reinforce each other to ensure robust protection of individuals in the digital age. Privacy is focused on the protection of one's private life, whereas data protection is aimed at giving individuals control over data that relates to them. For simplicity, this book does not differentiate between the two terms and refers the interested reader to this literature.

7.2 Why does privacy matter on mobile?

A powerful analysis of why privacy matters on mobile was published in a 2020 report Out of Control: How Consumers Are Exploited by the Online Advertising Industry by the Norwegian Consumer Council (2020). Over 186 pages, the researchers analysed the data practices of 10 popular Android apps. Amongst those apps were a children's app, a period tracker, and various dating apps. What they found was a blatant disregard for governing data protection legislation, including GDPR.

Grindr, a popular LGBTQ dating app, showed particularly troublesome data practices. The app was found to share users' exact location, IP address, phone ID, age, and gender directly with 18 third-party companies, including Google Crashlytics, Google Firebase, Tencent, Facebook, and MoPub. To make matters worse, many of these companies reserved the right to pass on this data to many others in a 'cascading data sharing' process. Consequently, potentially thousands of companies can access this private information. For example, MoPub alone listed 170 partners in its privacy policies with whom it may share data. One of these partners, AppNexus, reserved the right to share data with its 4,269 partners. Importantly, all these companies have their privacy policies, which commonly reserve the right to further sharing of personal data with partners. As a result, no one can know what is going on with the data in Grindr. Such data processing is fundamentally incompatible with the GDPR, not least the principle of transparency that requires individuals to know what happens to their data. This is impossible in the example of Grindr and countless other apps.

7.2.1 Real time bidding

MoPub in Grindr is a good example of what's going wrong with data practices in mobile apps. Its software provides real time ad bidding (RTB), which serves many mobile ads.

While the entire online advertising market is worth $240 billion, RTB only attracted $5 billion in spending (1.8 per cent) in 2018. However, RTB mainly sells low-quality ads and otherwise unused display space on desktop and mobile. As a result, the proportion of RTB amongst the overall number of online ads may be higher than 1.8 per cent.

In RTB, advertising space on a user's device is sold via real time auctions. The user (supply side) provides the advertising display space on their desktop or mobile device, while the advertiser (demand side) is interested in buying this display space and can place bids on it.

·Ad exchanges manage the auctions. In a nutshell, ad exchanges apply the concept of eBay to the online advertising space. The highest bidder wins. Prominent ad exchanges are Google AdX, Microsoft Advertising, and MoPub, as in the case of Grindr.

An auction proceeds as follows. The user's device requests an ad from an ad exchange, a platform for ad auctions. This request usually contains additional data, such as the visited website, user identifiers, the phone number, and the location. The ad exchange may enrich the data received from the user with further DATA and then contact interested bidders (bid request). The bidders receive this information about the user and may make a bid to purchase the offered advertising space on the user's device. Bidders usually have less than 100 milliseconds to respond, after which the auction ends. The highest-paying ad is shown to the user. The whole process from requesting to serving an ad takes about 200 ms.

RTB comes with severe privacy issues for the user. The actual 'supply' is the user data according to which the ads are served. As in Grindr, user data is regularly exposed to hundreds of advertisers, each of which can then follow users around the internet and build comprehensive profiles. This approach to online advertising also relies to a large extent on statistical inferences. These inferences are prone to false assumptions and may raise further issues, such as discrimination and outright harm (Wachter, 2019a). It has even been reported that intelligence services around the globe use location and other data obtained through RTB to trace subjects.

The questionable practices are being investigated by the UK Data Protection Regulator, the Information Commissioner's Office (ICO), which found that the companies responsible 'have their heads firmly in the sand' (Taylor Wessing, 2022). To date, there have been almost no tangible outcomes from this work, which is representative of the wider enforcement efforts by European data protection authorities. While the data protection laws on the books, first and foremost, the GDPR, are strict, there is almost no enforcement in practice. As a result, it is no wonder that the baseline for mobile privacy is rather disappointing.

7.2.2 Impacts of tracking on livelihoods

Even before the study by the Norwegian Consumer Council, Grindr had faced similar accusations over its data practices.

Back in 2018, Grindr was found to share medical information, including whether they are HIV positive or negative, when they were last tested for sexually transmitted infections (STIs), and whether they take preventive medication against HIV pre-exposure prophylaxis (PrEP), with two analytics companies. This data was shared alongside a user's location data, phone identifiers, and email address, which could easily reveal the identity and whereabouts of individuals. This is particularly troublesome because users share their health information on their Grindr profiles to protect other members against STIs.

Grindr maintained that they only shared this information to analyse and improve app usage, but ended this data collection in response to public coverage. However, sharing information about its users with third parties can put individuals at risk. Homosexuality is illegal in dozens of countries. In some of them, it may be punished by death. Along with the use of Grindr, an indicator of sexual orientation, may motivate discrimination or prosecution. If there are data leaks, commercial data deals, or warrants for data disclosure by authorities, this data, intended for analytics purposes only, might be used against the same users. Sharing data with third parties increases these risks further and commonly leads to uncontrolled further data sharing by these third parties.

Even in countries without repressive legislative regimes, people are put at risk. Some people prefer not to disclose their sexual orientation publicly and may face discrimination or other negative consequences. For example, in a case from 2021, a US-based Catholic priest and former general secretary of the US Conference of Catholic Bishops lost his job after he was outed as using the Grindr app by the Catholic news site *The Pillar* (Slate, 2021). Catholic activists had been able to purchase data about this priest from an online broker, which had obtained location records from Grindr. These records indicated that the priest had regularly visited gay bars in the past. According to *The Washington Post*, the Catholic activists spent at least $4 million to obtain this data (*The Washington Post*, 2023). Clerical ethics aside, this is an unprecedented case of private citizens weaponising personal data from commercial data brokers against other citizens. It also shows that most of our online activities can be traced when there is determination (and money).

For its mishandling of personal data, the Norwegian data protection authority ended up fining the company about €6.5 million. This corresponds to about 7 per cent of Grindr's global annual revenue and underlines the severity of the fine. However, Grindr still maintains that it would 'operate with industry standard practices'. This may be true, but it does not render this behaviour legal.

Similar extents of data sharing were found in many other apps. Tinder, a dating app, was found to share users' GPS location and 'target gender' with third-party companies. This and other information (including sexuality, political views, and drug use) was also shared by OkCupid, another dating app, with the analytics company Braze. Concerning data practices were also found in the analysed children's and period tracker apps.

7.2.3 Ubiquity of tracking and absence of choice

The continued ubiquity of invasive data practices in apps was demonstrated in my PhD research at the University of Oxford. Specifically, 2 million Android apps were analysed, 1 million from before (2017) and 1 million from after (2020) the introduction of the GDPR in May 2018 (Kollnig et al, 2021b). An automated scan of apps' *.dex files was performed (corresponding to the apps' program code) to identify all domains that are known to belong to tracking companies and that apps can potentially send personal data to. If there have been changes in the extent of tracking following the introduction of the GDPR, they should have shown up in our results.

Our results suggest that the GDPR has not had a large effect on the distribution of tracking across apps on the Google Play Store (as shown in Figure 7.2). For instance, 85 per cent of apps from 2017 could send data to Alphabet (Google's parent company), compared with 89 per cent in 2020. Overall, 43 per cent could send data to Facebook (now known as Meta) in 2017, and 38 per cent in 2020. The same handful of tracking companies have similar prevalence and prominence; the average app contains a similar number of trackers (measured at the level of companies rather than domains); and a consistent percentage of apps (15 per cent) contain more than 10 tracker companies.

Analysing a representative subset of the same apps in detail, it was found that hardly any apps fulfilled the legal requirements regarding consent in the EU and UK (Kollnig et al, 2021a). To this end, the legal requirements in these jurisdictions were analysed. It was highlighted that Article 5(3) of the 2002 ePrivacy Directive requires consent before storing or accessing information on a user's phone unless this is 'strictly necessary' for the operation of the service. Tracking is not considered strictly necessary, but it cannot work without accessing or storing information because it relies on singling out individuals. Therefore, it requires prior user consent in almost all cases of tracking.

Regarding the threshold for valid consent, the rules of the GDPR apply. This means that consent to tracking must be 'freely given, specific, informed and unambiguous' (Recital 32 GDPR). As such, tracking must pass a high bar. The requirement of being 'informed' about tracking is particularly challenging, if not impossible, for trackers to achieve in a data collection environment, in which data is commonly shared with dozens, if not hundreds, as in the case of the real time bidding of entities. In these cases, informing individuals and relying on consent is wholly infeasible.

Then, a random subset of 1,297 apps was empirically analysed from the larger dataset of 1.6 million Google Play apps from 2020, and each app

Figure 7.2: Prevalence and prominence of tracking companies in the studied apps

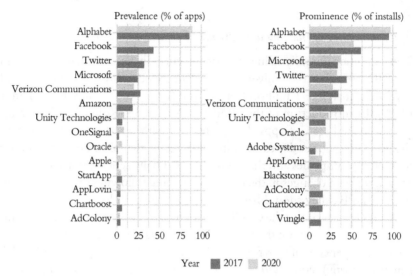

Source: Kollnig et al (2021b)

was opened on a real Android device (Kollnig et al, 2021a). About 70 per cent of these apps started sharing data with known tracking domains right at the first app start, before end-users could consent. What types of data were shared and for what purposes was not considered, and so it is not straightforward to tell whether some of this data sharing might have been 'strictly necessary' in the meaning of the ePrivacy Directive. Yet, this threshold is high and will usually not be passed by third-party analytics or advertising (Datenschutzkonferenz, 2019).

Investigating the apps further, only 9.9 per cent of apps asked for any form of 'consent' when starting the app. To increase the objectivity of the analysis, any form of affirmative user action was classified as consent, such as clicking a button or ticking a box. This definition is much broader than what EU law requires and thus only represents a minimum standard. When trying to refuse consent, about two-thirds of apps refused further operation. These apps are arguably not implementing 'freely given' consent, which underlines that the actual number of apps that comply with one central aspect of European data law is minimal.

In sum, the app ecosystem could be described as 'out of control', as termed by the Norwegian Consumer Council report. Data about most of us is widely shared, without our awareness (let alone consent), and commonly in violation of applicable privacy and data protection laws. Genuine controls and enforcement of the applicable laws are lacking.

7.3 A brief history of app privacy

7.3.1 What did privacy used to be before mobile?

It is worth reminding ourselves that privacy has not always been in the state it is now. Before the arrival of smartphones, many of the current data practices would have been deemed intolerable. Detailed data about individuals also happened to be much more challenging to obtain. Only with highly connected and sensory smartphone technologies did online advertising really take off. This is supported by statistics from the Interactive Advertising Bureau (IAB), the collective of online advertising companies, and PricewaterhouseCoopers (PwC) (see Figure 7.3).

The first boom of online advertising happened until the financial crisis. Revenues peaked at $23.4 billion in 2008 and fell to $22.7 billion in 2009. Once the crisis had passed, revenues rebounded and saw substantial further growth. Since around 2013, the market for desktop advertising has seen no further growth beyond the rate of inflation (approximately 2 per cent). Instead, the demand for mobile advertising has exploded and is now more than twice as large as desktop ads. This boom would not have been possible without Apple and Google turning a blind eye to massive illegal data collection on mobile.

The slow but steady erosion of our expectations around privacy and company morals is typical of surveillance capitalism and is an intentional business practice (Zuboff, 2019). After all, these companies are incentivised to grow the returns for shareholders and face limited scrutiny by regulators. This will be discussed more in Chapter 8.

7.3.2 The early days of mobile privacy

When smartphones first launched, they were relatively permissive regarding the access to data granted to apps. There are multiple reasons for this.

First, internet technologies, like the Hypertext Transfer Protocol (HTTP) or email, have traditionally been founded on principles of openness, collaboration and good faith. Only once these principles were abused did the industry adopt various countermeasures (for example, spam filters, denial of service prevention and 'I'm not a robot' prompts). Apple and Google embraced similar principles in the early development of smartphones. For example, Steve Jobs initially intended to rely on open web standards, instead of a centralised app store, to distribute apps on iPhones (Jobs, 2010). This did not come to fruition because a centrally controlled app store allows much tighter control of the app economy and higher revenues. Second, a permissive approach to apps' ability to access user data contributed to the early success of smartphone technology. For example, apps were not restricted from accessing users' contacts, calendar, or photos. Apple and

Figure 7.3: US online advertising revenues, 2003–2018

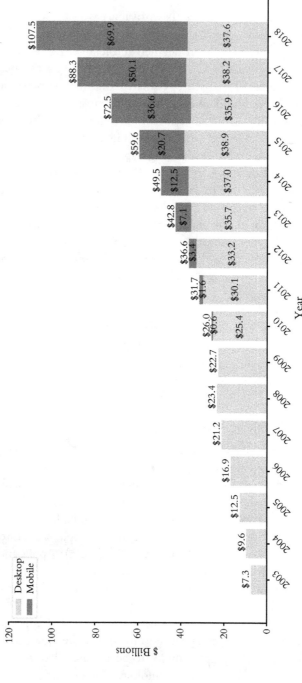

Note: Figures not adjusted for inflation

Source: Interactive Advertising Bureau (2021)/PwC

Google sought to lure developers into their ecosystems by making it as straightforward as possible to grow their businesses through ads and analytics. Third, in the Apple ecosystem, there might have been some misplaced trust in its review system. On the App Store, every app must be reviewed by a human tester. However, given the complexity of IT systems, it is impossible, even for a company like Apple, to inspect every single line of code of each submitted app.

As a result of these considerations, apps, once installed on Android or iOS, could obtain detailed insights into users' private lives. This included unique identifiers, such as a user's phone number and the device serial number, both of which cannot be reset by users (without getting a new smartphone or number). In addition, installed apps used to have unlimited access to users' contacts, calendar, photos, and further information. Only the access to other apps' data was limited since apps, on both Android and iOS, run in dedicated execution environments, also known as 'sandboxes'.

These assumptions were problematic, if not naïve or flawed. Some actors were not acting in good faith, too obvious privacy problems with apps might hurt Apple and Google's reputation, and Apple's app review was far from perfect.

The extent to which malicious data practices had taken hold in mobile ecosystems was impressively demonstrated by Yuvraj Agarwal and Malcolm Hall from UC San Diego in 2013. They developed ProtectMyPrivacy, an iOS app that allowed users to see a pop-up before an app could access their personal information. Because the app relied on modifying the iOS system, it was only available for expert users who had applied a jailbreak to their phones. Despite these limitations, the app was used by tens of thousands of individuals. This allowed the researchers to study the data practices of apps installed on participants' phones. Ultimately, the researchers gained insights into the data practices of 225,685 apps. Their research showed that access to the device identifier (48.4 per cent of apps), location (13.2 per cent of apps), contacts (6.2 per cent of apps), and music library (1.6 per cent of apps) was widespread in iOS and needed better protections.

Apple adopted much of ProtectMyPrivacy's functionality with iOS 6 in September 2012 (CNET, 2012). This was the first time that Apple implemented any pop-ups with regard to the access to sensitive information inside of apps. Apple also started phasing out the Unique Device Identifier (UDID), a permanent device identifier. This identifier had traditionally been important for advertisers and other tracking companies to analyse user activity across apps and build fine-grained user profiles of app usage. To replace the UDID, Apple integrated a secret tracking identifier into its iPhones in 2012: the Identifier for Advertisers (IDFA). Conveniently, the IDFA enables the same large-scale user surveillance that the UDID used to facilitate. Data-hungry companies could still engage in the same tracking of users' daily activities and build extremely fine-grained profiles about them. While it had been possible to opt out of the IDFA since 2016, this had to be done manually, and the option to do so was hidden deep in the iOS settings, an intentional choice by Apple.

Meanwhile, on Android, Google only introduced an Advertising Identifier in October 2013 (Google, 2013) and opt-in permissions in September 2015 (Google, 2015). It took the company even longer to phase out the Android equivalent of the UDID, the Android ID, from 2017. This reflects that Google, compared with Apple, relies much more on user tracking and advertising.

7.3.3 Google's acquisition of DoubleClick and AdMob

Barely noticed at the time but hugely consequential, Google decided to acquire AdMob for $750 million in 2009. Back then, AdMob was the most prominent advertising provider for mobile apps. As such, it represented a unique business opportunity for Google to grow the returns from its Android system by making it into an advertising machine.

Google additionally acquired DoubleClick for $3.1 billion in March 2008. The US and EU competition authorities investigated this acquisition at the time but eventually cleared it. While the authorities did anticipate privacy problems, they held that they weren't competition problems and thus not within their competency (Binns and Bietti, 2020).

Nowadays, Google has a monopoly over search text advertising and the intermediation of advertising, and it is subject to investigations across the globe. This has been confirmed in the US in two separate lawsuits (United States v. Google LLC (2020) and United States et al. v. Google LLC (2023)), which are both considering whether and how to break up Google. After all, Google owns most of the companies that are relevant for online advertising. This dominance allows the company to derive significant financial benefits to the detriment of competitors and consumers.

Interestingly, Apple was also interested in buying DoubleClick at the time but was outbid by Google (Business Insider, 2009). Instead, Apple bought the mobile ad network Quattro Wireless and launched its own ad network, iAd, a few months later (Business Insider, 2010). In 2016, Apple chose to abandon iAd and to prioritise other business areas. The iAd technology, however, remains the basis for ads in Apple News and App Store searches, as will be discussed in the following sections.

7.3.4 Recent developments and status quo

As a publicly traded company, Apple faces constant pressure from shareholders to keep growing its profits. Since revenues from the sale of physical devices have been stagnating, the company is shifting ever more into digital services.

Advertising space is one of the most lucrative such services and the foundation of Google and Meta's business models. This is why Apple now also focuses on advertising, having previously abandoned its iAd system in 2016.

The company has identified a strategic opportunity in providing ads, given its privileged position in the iOS and macOS ecosystems. Unlike its close competitors (such as Google or Facebook), Apple has not been subject to large-scale data scandals and enjoys much higher trust among consumers. At the same time, due to limited enforcement from public authorities, limited incentives exist to take user privacy seriously; therefore, Apple might get pressured by shareholders to develop more invasive practices over time.

The first step towards growing its advertising business was iOS 11.3, released in March 2018. This version of iOS introduced the so-called SKAdNetwork, which implements privacy-preserving ad attribution. Attribution is vital for advertisers who seek to track the conversion from an advert in app A towards installing app B. This can be easily implemented through the IDFA, shared by apps A and B, by sharing this identifier with the same remote server. However, the IDFA also allows the creation of detailed user profiles across apps, which is problematic from a privacy perspective. Instead, SKAdNetwork enables the tracking of conversions without sharing user identifiers with third-party companies (other than Apple).

In 2021, Apple started phasing out the IDFA (see Section 7.3.2). Its collection now requires app developers to seek prior user consent. This is implemented through a standardised consent screen as part of the ATT framework (see Figure 7.4).

The change in Apple's data policies was controversial and incited a fierce public clash with Facebook (9to5Mac, 2020a; 2020b). Facebook ran a public

Figure 7.4: App Tracking Transparency

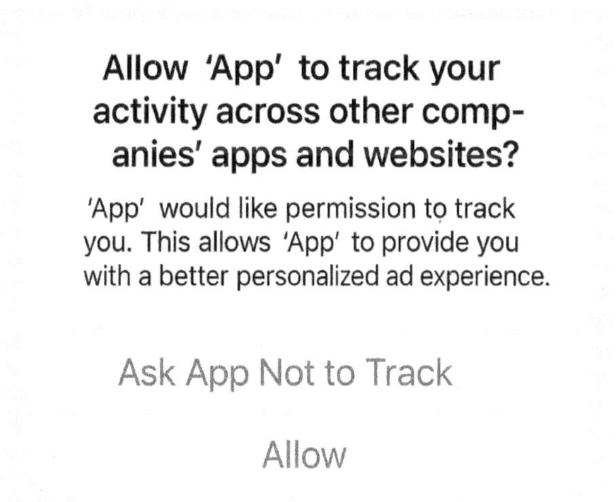

Allow 'App' to track your activity across other comp- anies' apps and websites?

'App' would like permission to track you. This allows 'App' to provide you with a better personalized ad experience.

Ask App Not to Track

Allow

smear campaign against Apple across leading US newspapers, in which Facebook argued that Apple's new privacy controls would disproportionately hurt small businesses. Coincidentally, the change has been claimed to have cost Facebook billions of foregone revenues (9to5Mac, 2021).

Interestingly, not only have iOS users long been able to opt out of the IDFA, but EU law has also, at least since 2009, required explicit user consent to tracking, as discussed in Section 7.2.3. This makes one wonder about the actual impact of EU laws on apps' data practices and why the mobile advertising industry had not been better prepared to comply with tracking restrictions and applicable EU laws.

Despite Apple's marketing, Douglas Leith from Trinity College Dublin found that an average idle iPhone shares data with Apple every 4.5 minutes (Leith, 2021). Android phones showed similar behaviour, except that they shared data with Google, a company that does not make similar claims about privacy as Apple.

My research raised further doubt about Apple's marketing promises, having analysed and compared 12,000 iOS and 12,000 Android apps (Kollnig et al, 2022a). iOS and Android apps were found to engage in many of the same concerning data practices. Violations of data protection and privacy laws were rampant in both ecosystems. For example, on both platforms, consent to tracking is commonly absent from apps, even in kids' apps.

Around the same time as the ATT, Apple also introduced so-called Privacy Nutrition Labels (see Figure 7.5). These are meant to give users easy insights into apps' data practices. However, the labels are self-reported by developers and not independently verified by Apple (see also Section 5.2.3). This creates the risk that the labels may show inaccurate information. This was confirmed through empirical research: discrepancies between apps' reported and actual

Figure 7.5: An example of a Privacy Nutrition Label, introduced by Apple in 2021

data practices are common. In collaboration with Netzpolitik, a leading German news organisation for digital rights, the nutrition labels of popular iOS apps were analysed (Netzpolitik, 2022). Overall, 22.2 per cent of the 1,682 tested and randomly selected apps claimed in their labels that they wouldn't collect any data from users. Closer inspection, however, showed that about 80 per cent of them did in practice, right after first opening the app and not further interacting with it. A prominent example was the 'RT News' app by the Russian state propaganda apparatus that claimed not to collect any data. Yet, when opening the app, the app, in fact, sent data to 19 different domains, including some that are linked to advertising purposes. Similarly, other popular news and games apps did not correctly disclose all their data collection practices.

That privacy on iOS is, to an extent, a marketing claim, was also demonstrated by Apple's announcement to restrict all tracking in children's apps in 2019 (TechCrunch, 2019). After this announcement, the company even updated its App Store policies and stated that 'Apps in the kids category *may not* include third-party advertising or analytics' (emphasis added). However, this policy never ended up being enforced. The policy change caused a significant backlash from the industry. Ultimately, Apple quietly changed its policies to 'Apps in the Kids Category *should not* include third-party analytics or third-party advertising' (emphasis added).

Interestingly, research found that iOS apps in the children's category can request user location much more commonly than their Android counterparts (26.6 per cent on iOS compared with 3.8 per cent on Android) (Kollnig et al, 2022a). As long as there's limited legal pressure, privacy protections for children will remain largely absent (*The Washington Post*, 2022).

In response to Apple, Google also introduced privacy labels on its Play Store. However, Google's policies have so many exceptions that the Play Store privacy labels could be seen as constituting end user misinformation rather than honest privacy disclosures. In particular, if information about data practices is disclosed prominently within the app, then these practices don't have to be additionally disclosed on the Play Store page. Hence, by design, Google's nutrition labels are never meant to be complete, unlike Apple's.

Overall, Apple and Google deliberately enabled the large-scale tracking of individuals because it allowed them to increase the adoption of smartphones and make more profit.

7.4 What's next for app privacy: no more tracking?

Over recent years, the pressure on tracking providers has been increasing. In February 2022, the Belgian data protection authority found that a key mechanism behind consent banners online, the IAB's Transparency & Consent Framework, is in violation of the GDPR (Gegevensbeschermingsutoriteit,

2022). Among other aspects, the authority argued that the IAB is responsible for this data collection as a data controller (for more details on the concept of controllership, see Section 4.2) and not just those organisations that use the IAB framework. This ruling by the authority represents one of the first applications of the CJEU's rulings on joint controllership within the context of web and mobile tracking (Court of Justice of the European Union, 2018; 2019). The ruling underlines that those who design the technical infrastructure behind the tracking ecosystem bear responsibility for their design decisions under EU data protection law.

Around the same time, the Austrian and French data protection authorities as well as the European Data Protection Supervisor found that the use of Google Analytics on websites can be in violation of the ECJ's prohibition of personal data flows to the US without sufficient safeguards (Schrems II ruling) (Court of Justice of the European Union, 2020). These rulings suggest that the widespread sending of personal data to the US, for example, for common user tracking by Google and Facebook, faces an uncertain future. Without a new, reliable regime for the transatlantic sharing of personal data, the current practice of tracking is unlikely to be sustainable for much longer for app developers. The processing of personal data will need to find ways to overcome the reliance on US-centred infrastructure (and the potential harm posed by US intelligence agencies accessing these servers). Whether the proposed EU–US Data Privacy Framework from 2022 is fit for the task remains to be seen. It appears highly unlikely to solve the genuine concerns of unrestricted surveillance of EU citizens by US authorities.

As discussed in Chapter 6, the use of tracking relies on the fact that many app developers need ads for monetisation. Conversely, ads are the primary reason for using invasive tracking technologies. However, the invasiveness of tracking, as well as recent rulings by European data protection authorities and courts, cast doubt over the current practice. While ads and the personalisation of such are often permissible, the use of invasive third-party tracking to support these technologies is often not. As a result, the link between personalised ads and tracking will likely weaken in the near future.

The industry is reacting to these recent developments and is working towards privacy-preserving advertising solutions. Apple and Google are increasingly preventing apps, and thereby third-party trackers, from accessing persistent user identifiers. Prominent examples are the introduction of the ATT framework on iOS (blocking access to unique user identifiers without user consent), restrictions on third party cookies in the Google Chrome browser (preventing websites from saving unique identifiers in cookies to track users across websites), and Google's introduction of a user opt-out from sharing personal identifiers with apps on Android. While these measures can increase consumer privacy, they might also put more power over user data into the hands of the digital gatekeepers.

Increased restrictions on user identifiers might shift the tracking ecosystem in the direction of statistical identifiers (for example, device fingerprinting). A company might then (likely wrongly) argue that these statistical identifiers do not fall under the protections of the GDPR anymore, since data cannot be uniquely attributed to an individual or only with great effort (Veale et al, 2018). This argument is already used by the industry to justify the use of pseudonymous identifiers, which, however, fall under the GDPR (Court of Justice of the European Union, 2016; Norval et al, 2018).[1] While the threshold for the GDPR not to apply is high (Veale et al, 2018; Wachter, 2019b), the increased use of statistical identifiers could make it more difficult for individuals to enjoy and exercise their data protection rights in practice. At the same time, statistical identifiers may simply not be a good enough replacement for persistent user identifiers (such as advertising identifiers). If tracking systems do not have access to persistent user identifiers anymore, this might not only inhibit data trading, but might also make some smaller tracking companies less viable and run out of business.

The case of SKAdNetwork (see Section 7.3.4), offering privacy-preserving ad attribution and moving away from user identifiers, shows that it is possible to build more privacy-preserving advertising technologies. It also shows that there is a risk that the shift towards more privacy will reinforce gatekeeper power and reduce competition around mobile ads. More competition around ads is usually a good thing for consumers because it will reduce the cost of ads and, as a result, the price of products they buy. Currently, we also have competition around tracking (surveillance) of users, since tracking still underpins much online advertising. The result of competition around tracking has traditionally been rather negative for consumers because it creates a race for building better profiles and collecting more data about individuals, thereby conflicting with their data protection and privacy rights, among others.

It might sometimes seem difficult to imagine how the genie could be put back in the bottle in the tracking ecosystem, given that the app ecosystem relies on the income generated from tracking. However, this is what Apple is currently attempting, phasing out mobile tracking over time and shifting towards more privacy-preserving advertising technologies. This makes technical changes to the tracking ecosystem more important than ever and will need further scrutiny in the future.

7.5 Incentives matter, but remain absent in privacy

Apple's shift towards becoming an advertising company, in the disguise of privacy, has attracted much controversy. It also visualises the struggles of a publicly traded company in protecting privacy while having few incentives to do so other than reputational considerations. These struggles have rarely been so apparent as in the US court case against Google's monopoly in online search, which revealed that Apple receives about a third of Google's advertising revenues on Apple devices (see Section 4.4). This makes Apple complicit in Google's exploitation of user data and attention.

Reputation often gets cited as a motivation for individuals to engage in 'privacy calculus' and make privacy part of their commercial decision (and for companies to implement good data practices in return). However, this is not the case in practice, as ample research in privacy economics has demonstrated (Acquisti et al, 2016). Instead, capitalistic incentives, over time, encourage the creation of ever better monetised and more tightly surveilled data ecosystems. As long as individuals don't have any genuine choice and existing laws aren't sufficiently enforced (partly over fears that it might hurt the economy), we will not see any meaningful change. We will have to accept the status quo. Importantly, consent to a specific app's data practices is a flawed approach and will never be more than an illusion of choice (Solove, 2012; Bietti, 2020); therefore, better solutions that move beyond information disclosures and consent banners are needed.

Accepting the status quo will also mean that we will create a more divided and more fearful society in which no one can feel safe online, and that will bring us closer to an Orwellian world. While the economic considerations for companies are intuitive, the established data practices are also, in many ways, incompatible with our fundamental rights and freedoms. They already have highly negative effects on our democratic culture. Without the advent of smartphone technology, we would not have been able to come here, a world of ubiquitous surveillance. The continuous and multisensory capture of our daily experiences is unprecedented and relies squarely on smartphones.

A different world would have been possible if Google or Apple had allowed more transparency into the data practices of apps and had forced genuine privacy protections through their app store rules and review. For example, for the longest time, Apple and Google have integrated explicit tracking functionality into their respective operating systems, for example, advertising identifiers, and have made research into app privacy more difficult than it needs to be, as will be explained in more detail in Chapter 5.

In the meantime, we will probably continue to live with vast numbers of mobile apps that violate applicable laws, including the GDPR, as has been found by ample previous research. In other words, significant risks will remain to the rule of law, a fundamental aspect of the law, in the app economy. If the gatekeepers took more proactive action on app privacy or at least made privacy analysis easier for researchers and authorities, this would partly be remedied. However, it is reasonable for companies to engage in their current actions as long as there are no incentives to internalise the externalities around pervasive data collection, and act otherwise.

8

Health, Autonomy, and Addiction

The hyperconnectivity of modern smartphones, having a strong and stable internet connection during usage, makes it possible to monitor users in near real time. This has created a wealth of new business strategies and is the foundation of both in-app ads and purchases. In both cases, there is a strong incentive to optimise app design for revenue. As found in previous work, both business models are similarly linked to detailed tracking of user behaviour and large-scale analytics (Kollnig et al, 2022a). To increase sales, tracking users almost always brings positive returns for companies since there is minimal enforcement against excessive data practices, even though such data collection is usually (partly) illegal. Because Apple and Google take a commission and are interested in the growth of their respective app ecosystems, it has traditionally been in the interests of both companies to avoid being too strict on apps' data practices and instead help app developers grow into lucrative businesses.

8.1 Smartphone addiction of the 'Anxious Generation'

An important facet in shaping mobile business models has been the release of *Hooked* (Eyal and Hoover, 2013). This book is sometimes called the 'bible' of mobile user interface design. It spells out how design elements can strategically be used to increase app usage time and, as a result, financial returns from users, primarily through ads and IAPs. The book translates decades of research in behavioural economics and psychology into accessible guidelines for developers on how to exploit the cognitive vulnerabilities of individuals and provide them with dopamine kicks such that they get 'hooked' to a product, but never enough. Eyal's ideology explains, for example, why apps such as Instagram and TikTok regularly show users content that they are not interested in. This turns these apps into slot machines that make users scroll and crave exciting content. Now and then, interesting content will appear, but it does not for the most part. It's a bit like when taking drugs (I've been told): they, too, give short-lived pleasure, but rarely more than that. Users will spend many hours in the meantime and see many ads as they go along.

The result of those design patterns is a loss of digital self-control, and sometimes even digital addiction. One often discussed example of end user behavioural manipulation is the so-called dark patterns to make some options more salient than others, for example, accepting or rejecting cookies online (Gray et al, 2018). Most will have experienced those cookie banners that commonly make the acceptance of cookies much more complicated than rejection, for example, using different colours, showing button sizes, or hiding the rejection option behind multiple clicks.

These are all examples of dark patterns commonly used to steer users in a direction that is beneficial for the developers of digital products, but is commonly less so. Besides forcing users into increased data collection, they are also frequently used to make users lose control over the time they spend on their digital devices, as this chapter will discuss in more detail. Loot boxes and virtual currencies, as discussed in Section 3.2.2, are other design elements that make users lose control over their spending and finances. These are, however, not commonly seen as dark patterns, underlining the difficulty of defining what constitutes harm in the digital space (Datta et al, 2022b).

Often, such design practices are already illegal under applicable laws, but enforcement of these laws is lacking. For example, when addictive design patterns are used in relation to personal data processing, then the GDPR (see Section 4.2) would usually apply, and the principle of 'fairness' in particular (European Data Protection Board, 2023). Making users lose control would commonly violate this principle. However, enforcement of the law keeps lacking (Massé, 2020; Irish Council for Civil Liberties, 2021; Kollnig et al, 2022a).

Sadly, the adoption of (addictive) smartphones has coincided with a steep rise in the prevalence of mental health issues, including loneliness, anxiety, depression, and suicide. This observation has been made around the globe. While it is difficult to establish causation, there seems to be little doubt that smartphones have played a role. Jonathan Haidt has provided the most coherent account of this in his book *The Anxious Generation: How the Great Rewiring of Childhood Is Causing an Epidemic of Mental Illness* (Haidt, 2024). One of his key observations is that the advent of smartphones has turned children's play behaviour upside down. While kids used to go outside and socialise with their peers in person, most kids now spend a significant amount of time in front of their screens and talk to people online via chat or video call. This creates immense peer pressure and makes it difficult for parents and their kids to withdraw from these trends.

Nowadays, children grow up in environments that are highly unnatural to anything we've experienced in the past. However, play is one of the primary forms of learning for children and an essential aspect of reaching maturity (Ginsburg, 2007) 2007). Then, it is no surprise to see such an increase in the prevalence of mental health issues. In response, many organisations are considering how to protect children from these trends, for example, by banning smartphones from schools altogether and imposing stricter age limits on the use of social media. Regarding excessive data collection, a notable intervention exists in the UK with the Age-Appropriate Design Code (AADC) from 2020 that provides a specialised and legally binding kids-focused version of the GDPR (Information Commissioner's Office, 2020); however, there is also a lack of enforcement.

What is bad for children often is not good for adults either. It would be naïve to assume, especially given the enormous power imbalances between app store providers and users, that adults have more control over their digital device use and are in a much better position to protect themselves against digital harms, including digital addiction. It is just that the consequences may not be as grave for those who have already grown up and established their sense of self and identity.

Despite these concerns, addiction to digital devices, for most people, is not an addiction in the same way as other addictions, like those to substances. Very few of us have a physical dependency on digital devices and can live without them for a while, for example, on vacation. However, our dependence on such devices, including a loss of control of our device use, is difficult to deny, motivating the need for closer examination.

8.2 App review and screen time

This status quo in mobile business models creates various negative effects for individuals, not least their health, autonomy, and development of identity, and children in particular.

As we move away from ownership offline and online (as discussed in Section 6.1), one of the most important ingredients for business in apps is time spent on the app, or more generally, 'app engagement'. The app Candy Crush, developed by Activision Blizzard, is a good example. It continues to be one of the most lucrative mobile games and uses ads and IAPs as part of its monetisation strategy. Regarding ads, the implications of more time spent on the app are relatively straightforward. If a user spends more time playing the game, then Candy Crush can display more ads to the same individual, which translates into increased ad revenue for Activision Blizzard. As for paid content, the app heavily uses time-based elements, where users can only play a limited number of games unless they pay. Because many users enjoy playing this game, this urges users to pay for the time spent on the app, which renders the monetisation strategy of Candy Crush akin to a subscription model. When I ask my dad about how much he's spent to date on Candy Crush, he has limited answers; keeping track of in-app spending remains very difficult.

Famously, Shoshana Zuboff termed this new business model 'surveillance capitalism' (Zuboff, 2019). This term refers to the commodification of user interaction with digital systems. Interestingly, Google and Facebook vehemently rejected advertising on their respective services in their early days. For example, Google claimed on its official blog: 'There will be no banner ads on the Google homepage or web search results pages. There will not be crazy, flashy, graphical doodads flying and popping up all over the Google site. Ever.' (Google, 2005)

This statement has not aged well. Today, Google Search and other Google services are full of ads. This is an important reason why Google was found to be a monopolist in the US search market in 2024. As large tech companies discovered (and this took some time) how valuable the data created by users was (that is, users' search history and social interactions), these companies slowly became some of the most lucrative advertising companies. At the same time, Apple's business is, at least for now, mainly focused on the sale of physical devices, and thereby not well described by Zuboff's theory. This highlights the need for independent study of the app economy, as performed in this book.

Zuboff (2019) anticipates that, in the future, users will be ever more determined by the predictions of algorithms rather than the other way around. This statement is a no-brainer, given that the extent to which societies rely on algorithms will only increase. However, the extent to which we are influenced right, as well as we will in the future, is less clear, especially if we manage to enforce stricter rules in the digital economy. It's in our hands.

Without mobile devices being designed as they currently are, large tech companies would likely make much less money. For example, Apple, for a long time, only allowed somewhat limited control of device screen time, unlike Android. In late 2018, the company even banned, based on privacy concerns, existing screen time apps from the App Store; coincidentally, Apple had only just introduced its own inferior Screentime app (*The New York Times*, 2019). This sudden move seems at least somewhat counterintuitive, given that it would imply that Apple's app review had previously been insufficient or that the evidence underlying this review changed significantly once Apple had developed its screen time app (although Apple also develops the underlying iOS ecosystem and should know the strengths and limitations of it in-depth). Since 2021, in response to legal scrutiny (TechCrunch, 2020a), Apple opened up its ecosystem to third-party screen time apps, which now resemble their Android equivalents (TechCrunch, 2021a). However, while solutions for fine-grained control of screen time exist on Android as third-party apps, they tend to be cumbersome to configure. Apple and

Google continue to have a strong interest in designing smartphones so that we spend more time on them (which translates into revenue for both companies) and will buy a new smartphone in the near future (which is the foundation of Apple's business model).

In fact, the observation that users need screen time apps in the first place is a sign of market failure, including failure of the app stores' app review processes.

Apple and Google impose a wide range of guidelines on how apps should be developed (more on this later in this chapter). Interestingly, there are hardly any restrictions on the use of engagement-increasing design apps in the app store policies of Google and Apple. Examples of these designs can be found in social media apps like Instagram, which use many techniques to increase the time spent on the app. Two examples are the 'pull-to-refresh' and the 'infinite feed' design patterns. Pull-to-refresh means that new content is loaded when pulling down at the top of the Instagram feed. If one does that on Instagram, one is usually shown a quick loading indicator and then a list of new content rather than just a few new posts. This turns the Instagram app into a gambling machine that randomly rewards users with dopamine rushes but often also returns a lot of garbage posts. Apple intentionally does not use this design in its apps since it's habit-building. Yet, it is not actively policed against in other apps either. Apple and Google even provide ready-to-use components for app developers to implement pull-to-refresh ('SwipeRefreshLayout' on Android and 'UIRefreshControl' on iOS).

The infinite feed, too, is common among social media apps and offers end users an endless supply of social media content when scrolling down the newsfeed. This approach can be problematic because users lose their sense of time and the amount of content consumed, unlike traditional list views on desktop and mobile that come with progress bars on the right-hand side. The infinite feed is often combined with the pull-to-refresh design pattern to undermine further users' sense of control and agency over their digital device use. With the RecyclerView on Android and the UITableViewDat aSourcePrefetching on iOS, infinite scroll now only takes a few minutes to implement for app developers.

At the time of writing, neither Apple nor Google includes general rules on engagement-increasing designs in its app store policies. This is unsurprising, given that Google's business model is tightly linked to user engagement, particularly on YouTube. On the App Store, apps in the Kids Category '*must not include* links out of the app, purchasing opportunities, or *other distractions to kids* unless reserved for a designated area behind a parental gate.' It's unclear what might qualify as 'other distractions to kids', which makes it difficult to enforce this rule meaningfully. Further, apps in the Kids Category are a very small minority, less than 1 per cent of apps on the app stores (Kollnig et al, 2022a). This is because signing up for this programme is optional for developers. As a result, many apps aimed at children are not part of the Kids Category and do not fall under these rules.

8.3 Loss of individuality and obsessive simplicity

Digital harms are one of the most apparent manifestations of an increasing loss of individuality and customisation in digital systems. Instead, mobile devices embrace simplicity, inspired by the Bauhaus movement of the 1920s and the industrial design of Dieter Rams. He was once the chief designer at the German consumer products company Braun and became the inspiration for Jony Ive, the former design lead of Apple.

A striking example of this trend towards increased, and almost obsessive, simplicity stems from the offline world. Since around 2017, major companies have increasingly embraced Apple's minimalist design, including in their brand identity and logos. Instead of embracing unique logos with a unique set of colours and typography, companies now usually opt for sans-serif fonts and a single colour in their logo design. Just look around you, and you'll notice, for example, in the logos of Google, Facebook, eBay, Yves Saint Laurent, Rimowa, and Jaguar.

Finding out about this wide adoption of minimalism across businesses and what it may mean for individuality and culture was an important motivation to pursue this book in the first place. It made me wonder, as rarely before, what role the decisions by the gatekeepers behind smartphones might have played in all of this. This question is, obviously, difficult to assess. Causality is incredibly difficult to prove, especially in the real world. It is impossible to dissect the brains of the lead designers behind the new logos and to trace how their thinking was tied to trends set by mobile devices.

What seems clear is that the ubiquity of mobile devices has played a significant role in choosing these new designs. The decision of Microsoft, Apple, and Google to adopt minimalistic design widely across millions of apps, through their technical components, design guidelines and app review processes, has only made this ubiquity of minimalistic design possible. After all, we are what we do, and many of us spend a lot of time on our mobile devices. This naturally primes our expectations in a way that we also expect similar designs in our non-digital space. Many individuals spend hundreds of hours each month looking at apps that must be designed according to Apple's (and Google's) minimalistic app design guidelines. Consequently, we should not be surprised that these companies play an important role in setting cultural norms and expectations in design.

One result of the current obsession with simplicity is a loss, to a degree, of individuality in our digital and non-digital worlds. Losing individuality means that we also lose an important aspect of our culture, which is what makes individuals more unique and represents an enormous source of creativity. Expressing our unique selves and developing our distinctive character becomes more challenging.

This is also reflected in the linguistics around the app ecosystem. In the pre-smartphone world, individuals were often seen and referred to as 'customers' by companies, thereby emphasising the financial nature of human beings. After all, they would usually retrieve products, including software, by physically purchasing them. App stores, online advertising, in-app purchases, and digital subscriptions had not been invented yet, at least not in the way we are currently familiar with them. These customers needed to be understood and catered to, and would often be involved in user studies or surveys about our wishes. Some form of humanity existed in our software design.

Nowadays, individuals are usually seen as mere 'users' who are at the mercy of software companies. Rather than having a name and personality, we are referred to and commodified through our cookie identifiers, online purchases, and browsing history. Instead of user studies, we are regularly subjected to A/B testing, trying to exploit our most primal behaviours. As such, we have come a long way from being 'All human beings are born free and equal in dignity and rights', as proclaimed in Article 1 of the Universal Declaration of Human Rights. Sadly, human beings are no longer equal but increasingly divided into a techno elite and the sheep that they nourish. This techno elite is reaping the benefits from the ongoing digitisation, while hardly giving back. This arises from the appalling operation of public digital infrastructure by private actors for disproportionate levels of profit.

Instead of being purely seen as commodities, we, by law, deserve to be treated as human beings and individuals, every one of whom is special and needs careful treatment. Individual autonomy needs to be protected to ensure that humans flourish. This is, however, incompatible with the current obsession with simplicity and trying to make everyone the same.

An important driver of this loss of individuality is the app store concept that imposes stringent conditions on how apps are made. As for the app code, Apple and Google provide a predefined set of APIs to allow apps to communicate with other apps and the operating system. Apps are usually made with the development tools provided by those companies, that is, with Apple's Xcode or Google's Android Studio, as discussed in Section 2.2. This approach represents a significant change over how programmes used to operate in the desktop era, in which much fewer technical constraints were imposed on programmes.

Beyond a higher degree of standardisation of the underlying technical components, mobile apps must also fulfil stringent design guidelines. These guidelines align with what Apple and Google implement for their own apps and aim to ensure a consistent user experience on each platform. These design guidelines are further supported through a range of premade design components for app developers to support the design process, such as infinite scroll and pull-to-refresh, as discussed in Section 8.2. These components represent a technical means to support the enforcement of the applicable design rules. Active enforcement of the design guidelines during the app review process complements the technical enforcement.

8.3.1 Underlying design philosophies

The design of mobile apps was substantially affected by the vision of Steve Jobs and his colleagues at Apple. Famously, Jobs proclaimed that 'People don't know what they want until you show it to them.' In other words, he held that Apple would always know better than the user and would hardly need to consult them when designing their technology. Jobs espoused market studies since they would only reflect the status quo of individuals' technical expectations and competence, but not give insights into the future of technology. Admittedly, Apple has been remarkably successful with its strategy, now being one of the most valuable companies on the planet.

This philosophy is, however, problematic for a global company like Apple. The belief that Silicon Valley workers would know what is best for everyone is unrealistic and flawed. Many of them stem from highly privileged backgrounds. They were lucky to receive some of the best education in the world at some of the best universities and now belong to the top 0.1 per cent of earners on this planet.[1] How can their judgement respect the unique sensibilities and needs of someone who experiences discrimination based on race, disabilities, socioeconomic status or otherwise on a daily basis?

As an engineer, it can be tempting to believe that the technology that you design is ethically and culturally neutral. After all, code, by itself, does not carry any value. However, the combination of many lines of code in computer programs, paired with the deliberate decisions around hardware and underlying infrastructure (such as the App Store), is highly subjective and value-laden.

Technology is deeply ingrained with the values that the developers of that technology embody and choose. This is demonstrated in Ruha Benjamin's book *Race After Technology: Abolitionist Tools for the New Jim Code* (Benjamin 2019). In this book, she makes the case that African Americans are currently underrepresented in the design of digital technology, particularly mobile ecosystems, and that this results in racial discrimination in the use of technology. In other words, the same racial discrimination exists in the offline and online world. One example is how Google used to label black people as 'gorillas'. In another case, Google Maps pronounced Malcolm X Boulevard, named after a famous Black US human rights activist, 'Malcolm

Ten Boulevard'. She argues that this would not have happened if African Americans were adequately represented in the design of those technologies.

As a result of Jobs' philosophy, Apple has long pursued a strategy that embraces design and simplicity in every aspect of its design. On its iOS ecosystem, Apple has been trying to control how the technology is designed in great detail, ranging from supply chains and computer chips to a proprietary operating system and a tightly controlled App Store.

Indeed, in the early days of modern smartphones, Android apps felt much closer to Windows Mobile or Nokia's Symbian because the operating system was initially developed as a rival to the incumbents. The original Android phone featured as many as 10 hardware buttons, cursor keys, and a physical keyboard for typing. By contrast, the iPhone had only four buttons and one switch (for muting).

Andy Rubin, one of the creators of Android, once described their vision as 'developing smarter mobile devices that are more aware of its owner's location and preferences' (TechRadar, 2008). This quote underlines the conflict in designing mobile devices that are 'smarter' (and more streamlined than previous devices) and allow for an expression of user preferences. It is in notable contrast to Jobs' philosophy.

As the competition around smartphone operating systems narrowed to two main providers (Apple and Google), the world has increasingly converged. Today's Android is tightly controlled by Google and more simplistic, while the iOS operating system features many more configuration options than it used to.

8.3.2 From skeuomorphism to minimalism

Touchscreen devices existed long before the iPhone, but had never reached mass adoption. As discussed in Section 3.1, Windows Mobile PDAs were some of the first widely used examples of these devices. They predated the iPhone and usually embraced a single-touch display combined with a stylus. The Nintendo DS used the same technology and approach. With this system, Microsoft tried to bring the familiar Windows experience to mobile. We now know that this approach did not work out; Microsoft eventually abandoned the market for smartphone operating systems in 2015.

There are many reasons why Windows Mobile failed. Important ones were design, navigation, and ease of use. Consumers were not used to touchscreen devices, and so, they first needed a helping hand to adapt. To make this transition from physical buttons and interfaces to digital ones more intuitive for users, Apple embraced skeuomorphism in its first iPhones. This is a design approach in which digital elements are made to resemble their real life counterparts. For example, the iOS notes app had a yellow notepad background and a leather binding, mimicking a physical notepad.

Figure 8.1: A calculator, which early versions of the iPhone mimicked to help users transition to touchscreen based navigation

Source: Flickr (Pinot and Dita, 2014)

In contrast, the buttons of the iOS calculator app were made to look like real buttons through the use of shadows and reflections. The calculator is shown in Figure 8.1.

As individuals became used to touchscreens and Windows Mobile had failed, Microsoft introduced its Windows Phone in 2010. Its design was characterised by the distinctive 'Metro' interface with large typography, flat icons, and solid colours (see Figure 8.2). This minimalistic design approach was in stark contrast to the skeuomorphic design that was prevalent at the time and was meant to set Windows Phone apart from other mobile operating systems.

The minimalistic design approach was innovative and well-received in some ways, but it was not without criticism. The simplicity and flatness of the design

Figure 8.2: The minimalistic design of Windows Phone

could be seen as lacking character and personality, and some users felt that the interface was, in fact, too plain and uninviting. Using similar typography, flat icons, and solid colours made it difficult for users to grasp information and distinguish between different apps quickly. The lack of depth and visual cues, in turn, made it harder for users to understand the structure of the interface and the purpose of different elements. These challenges especially affected those users who already struggle with using digital devices.

Despite the concerns attached to minimalism, Apple decided to adopt a similar approach, starting with iOS 7 in 2013.

8.4 Customisation and individuality in desktop and mobile

Before the advent of smartphone technology, desktop computers were the primary means of interacting with technology. For example, today, more than half of internet traffic stems from mobile devices; these devices only made up 6 per cent of global traffic in 2011 (BroadbandSearch, 2023).

8.4.1 Mobile versus desktop

A fundamental difference between mobile and desktop devices is the number of configuration options and user control they offer, thereby reflecting individual preferences. For example, the primary tools for photo editing on desktop remain GIMP and Adobe Photoshop. Both contain a great wealth of options for editing photos. It is possible to arrange photos across multiple layers, apply various filters and premade modification options, and export to various formats (see Figure 8.3). Meanwhile, the primary mobile app for photo editing is Instagram. The app's simplicity enabled the company to reach millions of users and to be eventually acquired by Facebook/Meta for $1 billion in 2012. Naturally, a wealth of other photo editing apps exist

Figure 8.3: Photo editing on a mobile, showing fewer options and being less powerful than on a desktop

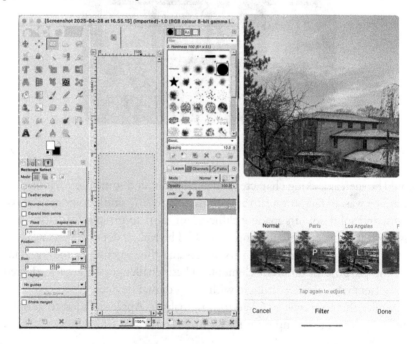

for mobile, some of which have more extensive functionality. Still, none compare with what is offered on desktop or are equally popular as Instagram.

In the past, the ability to modify the user experience significantly contributed to the success of Mozilla Firefox over Microsoft's Internet Explorer in the 2000s. It led to the emergence of a vast ecosystem of browser extensions to improve users' online experience. These extensions help end users remove malware from websites (for example, through tracker and ad blockers), reduce unwanted distractions and dark patterns (for example, by removing the Facebook feed and other distracting elements), make it easier for disadvantaged users to participate by allowing them to make the web more accessible (for example, through browser extensions that render any displayed text more readable for people with dyslexia), and enable platform workers to negotiate better work conditions. Similar functionality never took off in Internet Explorer, even though Microsoft tried to catch up, but it was too late. Recent versions of Internet Explorer, now termed 'Edge', rely on the code developed by Google for its Chrome Browser: the Blink browser engine.

The success of these browser extensions in Firefox was partly motivated by the fact that they were built on open web technologies, such as JavaScript, and were relatively easy to develop. Meanwhile, Microsoft promoted its proprietary ActiveX technology, through which it sought to monopolise web technologies, and eventually failed. Today, browser extensions are nothing more than HTML5 websites that are distributed to end-users through extension stores, notably the Google Chrome Web Store and the Mozilla Firefox Add-ons Portal.

Admittedly, desktops traditionally used to have more computing power, but this has changed with recent smartphones. Furthermore, the restricted display size and the focus on touchscreens make it more challenging to implement and allow similarly extensive configuration options on mobile devices than on desktops. As such, as much as mobile apps must follow the design guidelines imposed by Apple and Google, they also face different physical limitations and incentives.

8.4.2 Status quo on mobile

The two app ecosystems differ notably in the kind and extent to which they grant freedoms to developers and users of apps.

In the Google ecosystem, a relatively large amount of freedom has traditionally existed. For example, users have long been able to install apps from sources other than the Play Store on their phones ('sideloading'), with arguably positive effects for competition in the app ecosystem but also negative effects on device security (since sideloaded apps are often not independently verified) and app piracy (since paid versions of apps can easily be found online). Through an increase in Android safety measures (first and foremost, Play Protect) and adapted monetisation models (for example, ads and IAPs instead of paid content), developers have been trying to mitigate the negative aspects of sideloading, as discussed in Section 6.1.

Through Android's open source strategy, users have also long been able to produce modified versions of the Android operating system ('Custom ROMs') and thereby explore alternative software designs. Particularly in the early days of modern smartphones, a lively community of individuals existed who sought to challenge the values embedded in their smartphones and to expand and change their design and functionality.

Custom ROMs used to be popular with a significant share of Android users when, compared with today, the complexity of the operating system was lower (and contained fewer lines of code that needed maintenance), and Android functionality was more limited. Then, Google implemented almost no strategies to prevent the installation of modified versions of Android on smartphones. As a result, Custom ROMs existed that brought plenty of different alternative user interfaces (for example, bringing the iOS look to Android), contained fewer unnecessary preinstalled apps and custom components (which often introduce security issues, such as those from Chinese manufacturers (Gamba et al, 2020; Liu et al, 2023)), or came with better privacy protections (for example, GrapheneOS).

An interesting example of a Custom ROM was the TaintDroid research project by William Enck and colleagues (Enck et al, 2010). They sought to study the privacy properties of Android apps on Android Eclair 2.1 (released in 2009). This was motivated by the fact that the Google app store (termed 'Android Market' at the time) provided limited insights into what types of sensitive information apps can access. Therefore, the team set out to study the flows of sensitive data within an Android smartphone, from their 'source' (for example, the GPS sensor, the camera, or the phone contacts) to the 'sink' (for example, the internet or the SD card).

Many designs first trialled in such Custom ROMs have made it later to 'Stock' Android (that is, Google's version) and even iOS. Prominent examples of these are the ability to change the resolution of Android apps for increased readability (which first became popular through Paranoid OS), theming (which first became popular through CyanogenMod), and attractive lock screen widgets (as demonstrated by CyanogenMod cLock, which is now similarly adopted in iOS and Android). On iOS, ProtectMyPrivacy (discussed in Section 7.3.2) provided the blueprint for privacy controls on iOS and Android.

Today, many essential Google services do not follow an open source strategy and are the foundation of Google Ads and Analytics tracking on Android. However, without those, push notifications, GPS geolocation, IAPs, and other essential functionality do not function properly in many apps. This functionality is principally provided by the Google Play Services, proprietary software running on most Android devices. Furthermore, Google encourages the locking down of Android bootloaders, implemented a verified boot chain to prevent modification, and rolled out its 'SafetyNet' to prevent the use of sensitive apps (like those for banking, Snapchat and Pokémon Go) on modified devices. Some internet outlets even declared that Google's new changes might bring an end to Custom ROMs (SlashGear, 2020).

Google regularly claims that these changes would enhance device security, which is a common argument for restricting user freedoms. What is problematic about these changes, however, is that there was, as is common in the platform economy, no consultation of the affected users nor any accountable decision-making. Instead, Google just assumed that it was acceptable to roll out these changes across the world, thereby gaining even more control over the Android ecosystem than they already had.

In the Apple world, there was also a great interest in exploring alternative designs for apps and the operating system. The earliest versions of iOS came with barely any restrictions on installing third-party apps. As a result, the first 'jailbreak', called JailbreakMe, was introduced only a few days after the release of the first iPhone. This tool allowed the installation of arbitrary software on the iPhone, at a time when Apple had not yet released its App Store and was instead putting its hopes on web apps. The legality of jailbreaking has been the subject of extensive discussion and may vary across countries. Fortunately, in the US, as of 2010, an explicit legal exemption exists in copyright law that makes jailbreaking legal. Even outside the US, there are no reported cases of Apple taking court action against individuals who have used jailbreaks. Thus, jailbreaking should be considered as de facto legal.

A notable ongoing court case was brought forward by Jay Freeman. He published the first app store for iOS, called Cydia, in February 2018. Apple only introduced its App Store 4 months later, in July 2018. The case SaurikIT, LLC v Apple Inc. alleges that Apple abused its monopolistic power in the iOS ecosystem by establishing the App Store and preventing market access for Cydia. The outcome of the case still needs to be seen. Regardless of the outcome, new European legislation, particularly the DMA, now forces Apple to allow iOS sideloading and alternative app stores like Cydia. This has been discussed in Section 4.3.2.

8.4.3 The community strikes back, using the limited means available

Smartphones and digital technologies would not have become what they are without the influence of the community. However, the channels through which Apple and Google collect valuable feedback from end users are minimal. The same is true for other apps on the app stores, as anyone who's tried to contact customer support for a free app has witnessed. As it stands, there is, for example, no means for individuals to report issues with the Google Maps app.

Given the vastly increased complexity of modern smartphone operating systems, a return to the widespread use of modded and community-customised versions of operating systems is unrealistic. In fact, the modding community has professionalised itself, as seen by big community projects like Graphene OS or /e/, being custom, after-market versions of Android. This is good for consumers, promising a higher level of trust and security, but these modifications should have been developed in the first place.

The extent to which these modifications could be successful is, however, held back by the extent to which Google allows such modifications and enables compatibility with existing apps, including push notifications, Play Store access, and IAPs. The Google SafetyNet presents a particularly high bar, completely banning Custom ROMs from running some sensitive apps. Meanwhile, on iOS, the DMA will promote the influx of alternative app designs in ways that have previously been impossible. This will allow the development of new, innovative app solutions and help iOS somewhat catch up with Android in terms of customisability.

On Android, developers have long repurposed OS components in ways that have promoted customisability. For example, the AppBlock app uses Android's Accessibility API, meant to help develop software for those with certain sensitivities and needs, to allow users to control their device use better, for example, by blocking certain distracting websites. Another example is the Android VPN functionality, which allows users to connect to remote networks, for example, at their workplace or university. Some apps, like the Rethink DNS app, use this functionality to block network communications with advertising-related servers. Given that Google's business model is in ads, it has ramped up enforcement against these practices and has announced that it will ban these apps with fake VPNs from the Play Store from November 2022 (Claburn, 2022; Google, 2022). This does, however, not prevent individuals from installing such apps from outside of the Play Store; it only makes this more cumbersome and increases the likelihood that end users install malware on their devices if they install from the wrong websites.

Overall, a strong need remains for end users to make modifications to their digital realities. This is, for example, underlined by the author in Kollnig et al (2023). In it, among other things, individuals were asked whether they would like to make any modifications to their day-to-day apps and whether they would like such functionality. Overall, 85 per cent of survey participants expressed that they would like such functionality and came up with a broad variety of potential changes and improvements to their day-to-day apps (Kollnig et al, 2023). In the meantime, end users will have to live with what is expressly permitted, or at least tolerated, by the platforms. They remain able to change the terms of making such modifications at any time and have regularly done so in the past. Two important outcomes of this are apps that are more privacy-invasive and distracting than necessary.

8.5 A precarious environment for (children's) health

Google and Apple have strong incentives to increase digital device use since they both derive more revenue from this. As a result, it is unsurprising that neither company properly addresses addictive and habit-building patterns in their app review process. They even provide ready-to-use pieces of code to implement some of the most commonly used strategies to increase digital device use, including pull-to-refresh and infinite scrolling. This is despite the growing evidence that smartphones might be at the root of a range of negative effects, particularly for the mental health and upbringing of our children.

In the defence of Apple and Google, the policing of malicious design patterns in apps is, in some ways, more difficult than providing better privacy protections. When it comes to privacy, it is relatively easy for both companies to implement strategies to limit unwanted data collection. Some of these strategies include the implementation of permission requests when running an app (for example, to access the camera or calendar) or restricting apps' access to cross-app identifiers like the IDFA.

However, it is difficult to believe that our current situation is the best we can do. This is especially true, given that Apple and Google operate a human review of apps. This review could easily, at least for a certain number of the most widely used apps, check whether these apps implement any problematic design elements and, if so, ask for their removal.

There might be lots of debate on what constitutes a problematic design element. Indeed, much literature exists on online harms or dark patterns, but no definite definition has emerged. It is just very difficult to establish this. Yet, such a definition would not be necessary if app stores simply embraced a duty of care for their users and erred on the side of caution and the user if in doubt.

9

Smartphones on Wheels? Sustainability of and Beyond the App Economy

We now take a step away from the app economy. Instead, we turn towards how the principles underlying the app economy have changed the production of IT systems at large. A coherent theme across these sections is a mixed record in terms of sustainability. For example, while the technology behind apps is instrumental in developing and deploying modern electric cars, app-based software usually has a drastically reduced lifespan. This is partly due to the heavy use of degrading hardware components, such as lithium–ion batteries, but also to changed paradigms in software production. At the same time, the amount of e-waste has been increasingly fast. In 2022, it measured 62 million tons, up 82 per cent since 2010 (United Nations, 2024). Only a small fraction of it gets recycled, while the rate of recycling has slumped and has not been able to keep pace with the growth in e-waste (United Nations, 2024).

Compared with desktop computers, mobile devices come with a faster life cycle and incompatible software updates. This is especially true for Android-based systems, which usually do not allow updates unless they are purpose built for the specific device. This is in stark contrast to the paradigm behind desktop operating systems, such as Microsoft Windows, which built a one-size-fits-all software infrastructure. All updates were usually compatible with all devices. Even the latest Windows computers can still run software from the 1990s. Only with Windows 11, from 2021, did Microsoft slowly begin dropping support for MS-DOS programs, which date back to the 1980s. Such decade-long support is unimaginable in current mobile platforms.

Meanwhile, Apple products usually offer longer lifespans in terms of software support than Android products. However, unlike for Android, Custom ROMs, which can often extend the lifespan of Android devices beyond what was intended by the manufacturer, do not exist for iOS. Once Apple decides to end support for a device, it will become incompatible with ever more apps, usually only developed for the latest versions of the operating system. Moreover, Apple has a vested interest in replacing hardware regularly because it derives most of its revenue from this (instead of ads).

Even though most of Google's revenue derives from ads, this does not mean that the company has traditionally been a strong supporter of longer device lifetimes. After all, the attractiveness of the Android ecosystem relies on the support from third-party vendors other than Google, such as Samsung, Xiaomi, or Oppo. Those companies, unlike Google, tend to derive a significant share of their revenues from mobile apps from the sale of devices. This explains why Google, in the past, has not been pushing for more compatibility in terms of operating system updates. While Google launched various initiatives to increase such compatibility (notable Project Treble from 2017), these have never reached wide adoption. This might be slowly changing, with Google promising 7 years of software updates for its line of smartphones, the Google Pixels, starting in October 2023. Whether other manufacturers will follow suit remains to be seen. Given the economic incentives, this appears unlikely to happen. This is especially true because the Google Pixel series has traditionally been a niche player, with only around a 5 per cent market share in smartphones in the US (Statista, 2023e). Meanwhile, Apple's market share in smartphones is about 60 per cent in the US.

9.1 Electric vehicles: smartphones on wheels

Back in the day, the manufacturing of cars was a matter of great pride and ingenuity. Its core, the internal combustion engine (ICE), became a highly complex and intricate machine with hundreds of moving parts. To work efficiently and reduce emissions, these systems were finely tuned over many decades, with some success. Between the 1970s and 2010s, fuel efficiency doubled from 12.5 to 25.0 miles per gallon, CO_2 emissions halved from 700 to 350 gram/mile, and the number of road deaths plummeted (Business Insider, 2016; *Financial Times*, 2020b). Despite intense efforts, China never managed to match the expertise of established car makers in the ICE market.

In recent years, the automotive industry has been undergoing dramatic shifts. The pressures to reduce CO_2 emissions have led to the emergence of new challenger firms. These efforts are spearheaded by Tesla and Chinese companies, such as BYD and Wuling. At one point, Tesla's market capitalisation matched that of the next 10 most valuable car makers. These companies are currently revolutionising how we think of cars, being powered by electricity rather than fossil fuel. By the 2030s, many jurisdictions, including California and the EU, will ban the sale of new cars with an ICE.

The technical complexity of electric vehicles (EVs) is very different from that of ICE vehicles. They have much fewer moving parts, mainly consisting of a battery and an electric motor. However, EVs are not as such less complex. They rely heavily on advanced electronics and software systems. For example, the battery management system, which monitors and manages the car battery, is a vital component of EVs. Moreover, the development and manufacturing of battery cells, the heart of an EV, is a highly complex undertaking. Designing safe, durable, and affordable batteries continues to be one of the biggest challenges for EVs. As a result, the battery contributes up to half of the production cost of an entry-level EV.

These shifts in manufacturing are bringing huge economic reconfigurations. For example, in Germany, the sector for cars and car parts made up 19 per cent of the total GDP in 2016 but was already down to 15 per cent 6 years later in 2022 (Recruitonomics, 2023). Given the supply chain shifting away from manufacturing to rare metals and battery production, the German economy is on track to take a major hit from the automotive energy transition. In light of the competitive pressure, Volkswagen announced in September 2024 that it is, for the first time, considering closing factories in its home country, Germany (CNN, 2024). Meanwhile, China is on track to emerge as one of the main industrial winners from this change, given that much of the value added in EVs derives from the Chinese industry. The EU and US have responded with tariffs, adding a substantial financial burden to the clean energy transition.

Modern cars, including EVs and ICE vehicles, have sophisticated digital components, including advanced driver-assistance systems (ADAS), infotainment systems, and (semi-)autonomous driving capabilities. These add another layer of complexity to these cars. Given EVs' vastly reduced mechanical complexity, manufacturers will rely ever more on their software as a unique selling point rather than traditional measures like fuel efficiency.

Because of these shifts from traditional manufacturing to software engineering in car production, it could be argued that modern cars are a kind of smartphone on wheels. Indeed, they share many of the same hardware components, for example, advanced computing chips and battery technology, combined with similar software components. Modern cars are, similar to smartphones, equipped with rich sensory and communication technologies that allow them to react to unexpected traffic situations, receive over-the-air updates, and even communicate with each other. They have also been one of the key drivers behind 5G and eSIM technology, which are also shared with smartphones.

The similarity between modern cars and smartphones was further underlined by the shortages in computer chips during the COVID-19 pandemic. The pandemic led to a massive increase in working from home and the sale of digital products and services, as well as decreases in international shipping capacity. Partly because of the resulting chip shortages, global car production fell by 26 per cent during the first 9 months of 2021 (J.P. Morgan, 2023). Tesla had to delay the rollout of new products, including their Cybertruck and $25,000 car (CBS, 2022). Various car makers, including General Motors and Opel, had to stop production of several product lines entirely (James, 2021).

Not only hardware but also software-wise, modern cars closely resemble smartphones. For example, Tesla cars are run by a custom version of Ubuntu, a version of the popular open source Linux operating system. Also, Android and iOS are compatible with the Linux operating system. The infotainment systems of most modern cars support Apple's CarPlay and Android Auto, which bring the familiar Android/iOS interface to cars. They allow direct interaction with the apps installed on an individual's smartphone. Android Automotive, a version of Android, goes a step further and is installed directly in the car, instead of on an individual's smartphone. Many major car manufacturers (including General Motors, Volkswagen, BMW, the Renault–Nissan–Mitsubishi Alliance, but not Toyota and Tesla) have announced that they will base their infotainment systems on this type of Android.

While Android Automotive is free and open source, Google also offers the Google Automotive Services (GAS) to manufacturers, similar to its Play Services on mobile. These bundle Google Maps, Google Play, and other Google services, and might give Google vast data about the global car ecosystem. These insights, in turn, give Google an even deeper understanding of individuals' lives and may even help advance 'Waymo,' Google's line of self-driving cars. Even manufacturers that have not yet adopted the GAS, such as Volkswagen or BWM, have announced that they will operate their own app stores in cars. In this way, smartphone and car technology will become even more similar in the near future.

Meanwhile, Apple has long been rumoured to consider the launch of its own car series. Under the codename 'Titan', the company allegedly poached a large amount of talent from competitors in the automotive sector, to build their own self-driving car technology. Given the continued technical challenges around self-driving cars, which remain highly experimental, it seems unrealistic that Apple will launch its car offering soon. Indeed, in February 2024, it was reported that Apple had shut down its car development (Bloomberg, 2024a).

9.2 Mobile technology on desktop

Before smartphones came along, laptops aimed to provide cutting edge computing technology on the go. Laptops shared many of the same features with their immediate predecessor, the desktop computer. They usually came with plenty of USB ports, a Video Graphics Array (VGA) monitor connector, a CD drive, and an ethernet port for a stable internet connection. Many of the internal components, including the hard drive and battery, were replaceable, just as they were on desktop. Laptops regularly weighed more than 3 kg. Even the MacBook Pro 2007 was 2.45 kg. It probably saved some regular business travellers the need for any other regular exercise.

Almost exactly a year after the release of the first iPhone, Apple started, yet again, to challenge established wisdom in the technology sector. With the release of the first MacBook Air in 2008, the company began setting the vision for modern laptops. The Air lacked an optional drive, featured a single USB port, and only had 80GB of storage. Despite all this reduced functionality, Apple charged a whopping $1,799 for the cheapest model ($2,540 in 2023 dollars). An upgrade to a faster Solid-State Drive (SSD) hard drive added another $1,000. Commentators at the time considered the device revolutionary but also criticised the Air's slow performance. In addition, the laptop measured only 1.93 cm at its thickest and weighed 1.36 kg. The battery lasted about 5 hours and, unusually, could not be replaced, as is the case for many smartphones. The Air was a huge commercial success.

The next big innovation in the laptop space was the introduction of the Chromebook in 2011. Motivated by the success of its Google Chrome browser, first released in 2008, Google presented a novel philosophy to laptops, one that focused mainly on the Chrome browser. At its launch, the installation of traditional desktop programs was not possible. Instead, so-called 'web apps', including Google Docs and Google Keep, could be stored for offline use but would still run in the browser. Recent Chromebook versions are directly compatible with Android apps (since 2017) and traditional Linux programs (since 2018). Due to low hardware requirements and price, Chromebooks are particularly popular in the education market and, for the first time, outsold MacBooks in 2020.

The most significant turn in bringing mobile technology to desktop have arguably been Apple's M chips, the CPUs (see Chapter 2 for an explanation of CPU) that run the latest iPads and Macs. Frustrated by issues with Intel CPUs, which had traditionally powered Windows and Mac computers, Apple decided to develop its own CPU. The architecture for this CPU was not entirely novel but rather heavily based on previous designs of iPhone CPUs. Ever since the release of the first iPhone, Apple has designed these chips in-house and contracted another company to manufacture them. The chips were initially manufactured by Samsung, one of Apple's direct competitors in the smartphone market. Later, Apple shifted to TSMC, which today is the largest manufacturer of the most powerful CPUs.

The shift away from Apple is significant because Intel uses a fundamentally different computing architecture than Apple's chips. Rather than running Intel's x86 instruction set, Apple's chips are based on the ARM instruction set. These instruction sets describe how apps and programs communicate with the CPU. One of the main differences between x86 and ARM chips is ARM's use of a reduced instruction set computing (RISC) rather than complex instruction set computing (CISC). In the RISC architecture, all instructions take one CPU cycle to execute, whereas CISC instructions may take multiple cycles. As a result of this reduced complexity, RISC architectures tend to consume fewer resources and have been more suitable for early smartphones. Most smartphones, on Android and iOS, rely on ARM designs. ARM is licensed by the UK-based Arm Ltd and can be configured to the specific needs of smartphone manufacturers. Arm Ltd does not produce chips; instead, this is done by companies such as Samsung and TSMC that pay for ARM's CPU designs. Meanwhile, Intel traditionally has not licensed its chip design to other chip designers, tried to build general-purpose chips that would work across a range of scenarios and manufacturers, and produced its chips in-house. As a result, it has been much slower to innovate.

When the Apple M1 chip was first released for Macs in 2020, it was the first chip to use the new 5 nanometer chip design. At the time, Intel was still using the 10nm design, while many other TSMC chips had already been using the 7nm design for a few years. Smaller chip design allows higher transistor density and computing speed while reducing energy consumption. According to Apple, the MacBook Pro with the new chip offers 2.6 times the computing power than the Pro with an Intel chip and doubles the battery life from 10 to 20 hours. Independent tests largely confirmed the superior quality of the new chip. Thanks to a special instruction set on the new CPUs and the Rosetta 2 software compatibility layer, x86 Mac programs will continue to run on ARM Macs for the foreseeable future, with limited losses in terms of computational efficiency.

Microsoft has long been trying to adapt Windows from x86 to ARM chips. Its first attempt was 'Windows 8 RT', dating back to 2012. These efforts, however, failed miserably due to a lack of compatibility with previous Windows programs. This, in turn, made Windows RT hugely unpopular with consumers, and it was discontinued starting in 2016. In 2018, Microsoft began a new attempt with its 'Windows on ARM', which has, unlike Windows RT, full compatibility with traditional x86 programs. Windows on ARM, however, remains somewhat experimental (including the support for some x86 programs), which underlines the extreme technical challenges related to changing the instruction set and makes Apple's successful change only more impressive.

The change of personal computer hardware and software architecture to something more similar to what is used by iPhones and iPads underlines the extent to which smartphones and mobile devices have driven recent computing innovations. Unlike at the beginning of smartphones, desktop computers now run off mobile technology more often than vice versa.

9.3 Smartphone technology is everywhere

The car industry, being at the forefront of tackling climate change, and personal computers are just two types of technology that run on top of technology heavily inspired by smartphones. A range of further lines of technology use a similar hardware and software stack.

9.3.1 Tablets and e-readers

While Apple first released the iPhone, the iPad had been in development for much longer. Already in 1983, Steve Jobs had declared that:

> Apple's strategy is really simple. What we want to do is we want to put an incredibly great computer in a book that you can carry around with you and learn how to use in 20 minutes … And we really want to do it with a radio link in it so you don't have to hook up to anything and you're in communication with all of these larger databases and other computers. (The Next Web, 2012)

This vision, notably, was expressed by Jobs even before the World Wide Web had been released, which developed a methodology to link up all the 'databases' on the internet. It took Jobs 27 years to realise his vision, including departing temporarily from Apple, launching Disney Pixar, and developing the NeXT personal computer (the foundation for the MacBook, the iPhone, and iPad).

Given the engineering difficulties of building a large, multi touch device, like an iPad, Apple engineers eventually focused on a smaller device first, which became the iPhone. However, the original focus on building a powerful, portable computer was not forgotten. The iPad was eventually released in 2010.

Google tried to follow suit with its Android, but never caught up. Android tablets predate the iPad. For example, the Archos 5, released in 2008, was a 4.8-inch tablet running Android 1.6. However, the operating system was not made for the larger screen size, which made it a disappointing experience for consumers. Google tried to address this with the release of Android 3 (codenamed 'Honeycomb') in February 2011, a special version of Android aimed at tablets. It was also the first Android version to adopt the more minimalistic 'Holo' design. Devices with smaller screens would still run on Android 2 for some time, until Android 4 (codename 'Ice Cream Sandwich') from October 2011 tried to merge Android's phone and tablet versions.

Android 3 Honeycomb was notoriously buggy and had poor usability compared with the iPad; also, follow-up Android versions never fulfilled consumer expectations. The diverging strategies and designs for mobile and tablet further discouraged the development of tablet-optimised apps for Android and, thus, the adoption of Android tablets. Ever since the release of Honeycomb, Google has never made much effort to promote a tablet version of Android. The iPad was just too good and far ahead in terms of development and technical sophistication.

Also, as discussed in previous sections, iOS has traditionally focused on productivity, premium users, and high-quality paid apps. In contrast, Android has focused much more on gaming, mobile advertising, and freemium apps. Because tablets emphasise productivity, the Apple ecosystem had a natural advantage for this product category.

A special type of tablet is an e-reader. They have many of the same components as tablets, with the main exception being a black-and-white e-ink display that allows for a better reading experience. While early versions, such as the Amazon Kindle, came with a full QWERTY keyboard, this has been replaced with multitouch screens. Some e-readers like Barnes & Noble's Nook and Onyx BOOX even run on variants of Android. The most famous e-reader, the Amazon Kindle, does not run on Android, nor does one of the fiercest competitors, the Apple iPad. Both are, however, Linux-compatible, just like Android devices. This underlines that, in terms of hardware and software architectures, all e-readers are relatively similar. However, they cannot drive a car (yet).

9.3.2 Smartwatches

The first successful smartwatch was the Pebble. It was launched in 2013 following a successful campaign on the crowdfunding platform Kickstarter. However, the company had to file for bankruptcy only 3 years later. Millions of Pebble smartwatches were suddenly redundant because the company had to shut down its online servers, which were necessary to operate the watches. This serves as a cautionary tale for the difficulties faced by newcomers when breaking into the lucrative tech market dominated by a few companies, as well as the continued creation of large amounts of electronic waste resulting from products that are not meant to last.

Nowadays, both Google and Apple operate variants of their mobile operating systems for smartwatches: Wear OS (previously Android Wear) and watchOS. Similar to tablets, they've had different levels of success. Wear OS, originally called 'Android Wear', was first announced in April 2014 and was based on Android 4.4. Like Android for tablets, it never turned out to be a massive success. The small batteries of smartwatches were unable to provide enough power for the relatively battery-hungry Android. Also, the connection with smartphones, a necessity to use the full functionality of smartwatches, was unreliable, given the large number of different Android versions and manufacturers.

The Apple Watch was launched much later, in April 2015. Unlike Wear OS, it is only fully compatible with iPhones (not Android phones) and benefits from a close integration with the Apple ecosystem.

However, Apple wasn't entirely new to the smartwatch market at the time. Through its iPod music players, the company had already developed smaller watch-like hardware for many years. This is particularly true for the iPod Nano 6G and 7G, which were both based on a custom version of iOS. Indeed, the iPod Nano 6G, released in 2010, functioned and looked much like a watch, due to its rectangular shape and the ability to choose watch faces.

These devices struggled for a long time because they had relatively small batteries and would run out quickly if the display was turned on. By improving the software over time, Apple learned important lessons for the design of the Apple Watch. While Apple discontinued the iPod in 2022, its spirit has been argued to live on in the Apple Watch (ScreenRant, 2022). Nowadays, Apple Watch has the largest share in the market for smartwatches (30.1 per cent in 2021); Samsung, ranked second, only had a share of 10.2 per cent (Statista, 2022b).

9.3.3 Smart TVs

Android TV, an adaptation of the Android operating system, powers many smart TVs and streaming boxes. Similarly, Apple's tvOS, a version of iOS, is the foundation of Apple's Apple TV streaming box. In the Smart TV sector, Android can play to its strengths, being easily adaptable to the wishes of various device manufacturers. Battery consumption is not usually an issue in the TV sector, unlike with smartwatches. Meanwhile, Apple does not produce its own TV; it only produces a media box called Apple TV.

Interestingly, neither Apple nor Google is a market leader in the TV sector. In 2024, the most widely adopted operating systems for smart TVs were Tizen (12.9 per cent), Hisense VIDAA OS (7.8 per cent), LG Web OS (7.4 per cent), Roku TV OS (6.4 per cent), Amazon Fire OS (6.4 per cent), and Google Android TV (5.9 per cent) (CEPRO, 2024). These statistics show that the TV market is highly competitive and diverse. There is no single market leader, and many different approaches exist to making TV apps available. Indeed, open standards have played a significant role, with video apps such as Netflix and Amazon Prime being available across these platforms as apps based on the technical standards behind the web.

Something else stands out. The two most prominent operating systems, Tizen and WebOS, actually emerged on mobile. Tizen emerged from the 'Mobile Linux' project. This became the foundation for 'MeeGo', the smartphone operating system of the once largest mobile phone manufacturer, Nokia, before the company switched entirely to Windows Phone in 2011. The legacy of Nokia, which does not produce phones anymore, continues with Tizen, now developed by Samsung. Being one of the two largest phone manufacturers (besides Apple), Samsung has strategically been trying to foster its independence from Google by developing an alternative smartphone operating system. The company used Tizen in its smartwatches and smartphones for a while, but it has now shifted to Android variants. In its Smart TV range, however, Samsung still primarily uses Tizen.

Similarly, WebOS was initially developed by Palm, which used to be the leading developer of smartphones besides BlackBerry, before the arrival of the iPhone. Among other aspects, it was the first smartphone operating system that supported switching between multiple apps without closing them (multitasking). Released in January 2009, Palm's multitouch smartphones proved a commercial flop. Hewlett-Packard (HP) quickly acquired the company in April 2010, but neither company managed to compete with Apple or Google's app ecosystems. HP eventually sold WebOS to LG in 2013, who have since used it for their smart TVs.

9.3.4 Gaming and VR

The gaming sector is one of the most important markets for Android, much more than iOS. As a result, it is not surprising that a range of gaming consoles have been designed based on Android. Examples of this are the Ouya (released in 2012 after a highly successful Kickstarter campaign but discontinued in 2019), the Nvidia Shield (released in 2015), and the Logitech G Cloud (released in 2023). Nintendo's Switch, while it is not directly based on Android, contains Android components, including its multimedia and graphics technology.

Many have long predicted that VR would be the next logical step for gaming. This, however, has so far not happened, at least not widely. Mark Zuckerberg's Meta (the parent company of WhatsApp, Facebook, and Instagram) has famously been trying to facilitate this breakthrough by launching the metaverse and renaming his Facebook company Meta. Oculus, now part of Meta's Reality Labs, has been the core of this vision ever since Facebook acquired the company in 2014. Android, to this day, provides the software foundation for Meta's VR business. Despite billions of dollars of investment into VR, Facebook has so far generated hardly any revenue from Oculus. Meta's metaverse is considered to have failed. For example, it has been reported that Decentraland, a key metaverse platform, registered a mere 38 daily active users in 2023 (The Nation, 2023). Furthermore, a feature meant to incentivise users on Meta's premier product, Horizon Worlds, generated no more than a global revenue of $470.

Despite Meta's challenges in bringing VR to market, Apple has also entered the arena with its Vision Pro. Priced at $3,499 and with a battery life of about 2 hours, this new product is not aimed at a broad market but rather at developers seeking to innovate on this new platform. The software behind the Vision Pro, called visionOS, is yet again based on iOS.

9.3.5 Other Internet of Things devices

As computing hardware is becoming ever cheaper, an increasing number of devices, other than personal computers and smartphones, are connected to the internet. These devices include smart TVs, smartwatches, modern game consoles, as well as various other devices. This trend has been termed the IoT.

The IoT devices have been discussed in much other work, and the full coverage of these devices would exceed the scope of this book. It stands out, however, that Android is the foundation for many of these IoT devices. Besides the already mentioned devices, Android is popular in smart home devices (for example, internet-connected plugs, light bulbs, switches, thermostats, and security cameras), smart displays (often powered through the, now discontinued, Android Things OS), and smart appliances (for example, smart refrigerators, ovens, and washing machines) (Gadgets 360, 2013).

Android and iOS are also popular in point-of-sale (POS) systems that facilitate payment at small independent merchants, like the local cafe. An example of this is the Square Point of Sale system.

While not all these IoT devices run on Android (or iOS), they are usually deeply integrated with Android or iOS smartphones and can be controlled by them.

However, Android, as discussed before, comes with limitations. It remains relatively resource-hungry, both in terms of energy and computing needs. This makes it challenging to develop Android-based IoT products at a low cost. Google tried to establish a dedicated variant of Android for IoT, called Android Things, from 2015, but chose to discontinue this system in 2020 (Ars Technica, 2020). Other operating systems are simply more suitable for many IoT applications, particularly Linux- or Arduino-based ones. Indeed, in its own Nest smart home devices, Google deployed its new Fuchsia OS (Ars Technica, 2022), which has been speculated to serve as a playground for rethinking Android from scratch and potentially replacing it in the future (9to5Google, 2022).

Despite all of this, in the future, the reach of Android and iOS is likely to expand further with the further rise of IoT devices, as ever more devices become 'smart' and interconnected.

9.4 Warfare and industrial applications

This chapter has mainly focused on consumer-focused applications. They also have wider applications, such as in industrial settings. For example, under the term 'Industry 4.0', one commonly describes the hyperconnected factory of the future, in which sensors and internet connectivity allow better monitoring of components and production life cycles and, thereby, increase overall factory output.

Perversely, the same technologies that are widely used in consumer applications – making our lives more comfortable – have become unthinkable in modern warfare, thereby actively harming lives. Russia's illegal war against Ukraine, and the fall of the Assad regime in 2024, were among the first wars that used drones in great numbers. The success of drones also derives from the advances in portable computing. Like smartphones, they feature a small but powerful computing chip, high-definition camera, high-speed connectivity via Wi-Fi and Bluetooth, GPS geolocation, lithium-ion battery, and sensors like a gyroscope and accelerometer, in addition to rotors and additional weapon systems.

The most popular drone is the DJI Mavic (Reuters, 2024c). Produced at a great scale in China, it costs only between $1,500 and $3,000. This is a stark difference from previous military drones. For example, the RQ-11 Raven drone of the US military costs tens of thousands of US dollars. Due to its low cost and easy availability, the Mavic is, even though aimed at consumers, widely used by both the Ukrainian and Russian military. In terms of technology, the Mavic runs on an ARM-based CPU in the same way that modern smartphones do.

Each drone needs a human operator who is usually 2–5 km away from the front line and sees a continuous livestream video from the drone. This allows both the gathering of intelligence and precision strikes with small bombs at the enemy. The need for a constant link with a human operator also creates the main weakness of the Mavic and, indeed, most drones. As a countermeasure, both the Russians and Ukrainians increasingly use electronic warfare systems. These send out radio frequencies that interfere with the drone's connectivity to the human operator. However, this requires knowledge of the precise frequency at which the drone operates. This creates a cat-and-mouse game between drone operators and electronic warfare systems when changing the frequencies for communication.

In response, countries are hoping to build drones that are entirely autonomous and no longer rely on a connection with a human operator. Recent advances in AI and automated image processing are particularly promising to that end. It also brings us ever closer to warfare, where autonomous killing machines dominate. Utopia is knocking at our doors.

Interestingly, another counterstrategy against drones is Ukraine's 'Sky Fortress' that distributes hundreds of smartphones across the battlefield to detect unusual sounds that correspond to drones. This, also relies on AI capabilities and shows the direct impact of cheap smartphone technologies on warfare.

The in-depth discussion on industrial and warfare applications goes beyond this book's scope. However, they underline how widely portable computing, first and foremost, smartphones, has changed societies in the past decade or two.

9.5 Big tech moving fast into new sectors, even warfare

Smartphone technology, both its software and hardware, has completely changed the paradigm of how cutting edge software and hardware are created nowadays. The increased digitisation of everyday products has also brought several significant challenges that are shared with smartphones. As devices are always connected to the internet and share many of the same software components, this creates vast opportunities for criminals who seek to produce malware for profit or even to undermine national security by spying on arbitrary citizens. This makes it crucial for consumers to always run the latest updates on all their internet-connected devices and also makes consumers reliant on companies providing software updates across the lifespan of products. However, too often, devices are discontinued after several years, even though the hardware is still good to use. Due to a lack of public documentation and restrictions on independent repair, maintenance beyond what device manufacturers anticipate is often impossible. The increased digitisation of everyday products has also created rich possibilities for state surveillance, for which robust protections are still absent.

These choices are by design. iOS, Android, and most of the other mentioned devices are based on open source technologies. These could, in theory, facilitate community efforts and independent repair. Likewise, it is difficult to understand why smart speakers, refrigerators, and so on have to collect as much data as possible, at all times. A widely discussed study showed that Amazon Alexa speakers passively listened to interactions and shared this data with advertisers (Iqbal et al, 2023). A first step to remedy this would be much richer documentation obligations (both as they pertain to hardware and software), support for independent maintenance (including parts and manuals), and easy-to-use abilities for independent inspection of smart devices. Importantly, these facilities commonly already exist at the companies. There are limited reasons why they should not be opened up. The EU legislator is trying to access these issues, with better repair and data access obligations. Sadly, limited ideas remain to ensure compliance with these norms, and, likely, the same level of non-compliance as with data protection and privacy laws will be repeated in these new laws.

Finally, in response to Trump's re-election, the tech CEOs have been becoming very cosy with him and made major donations to his inauguration fund. While tech used to be a Democratic stronghold, norms have shifted tremendously. This also means that the relationship with the lucrative defence industry will be revisited (*Financial Times*, 2024). Smartphone technology already lies at the heart of drone technology, and it would not be surprising to see more involvement of big tech in this sector.

PART III

Conclusions

10

How Apple and Google Exert Their Dominance over Society

In light of limited past comprehensive scholarship on app store power, this book now tries to describe how influence unfolds in this space and propose a framework to this end, combining the findings from the earlier chapters. This framework is visualised in Figure 10.1.

There are at least three important layers to the power that Google and Apple exert in their respective ecosystem. At the core of this power are certain core values behind these companies. These values, in turn, translate into specific behaviour by the companies, which can lead to (systemic) risks and outcomes, as this book has emphasised.

10.1 Core values underpinning Apple and Google's decisions

The core values that stand out as drivers of Apple and Google's behaviour are Anglo–libertarian morals, shareholder value, and technological edge, intertwined with tech solutionism.

With the app economy primarily being designed in Silicon Valley by a set of privileged, high-paid engineers and executives, the fact that the values of this elite, often Anglo–libertarian ones, have an essential role to play in the platforms' behaviour comes as no surprise. These norms are reflected in statements by Steve Jobs that 'we believe we have a moral responsibility to keep porn off the iPhone'. (CNET, 2010) Based on this argumentation, the apps from notable newspapers were previously made unavailable on the Apple App Store because they showed naked skin, which is much less controversial in countries like France or Germany. This is often paired with a feeling of (moral) superiority, as highlighted in statements like 'People don't know what they want until you show it to them' by Steve Jobs. Chapter 6 (on monetisation and content moderation) and Chapter 8 (on health and autonomy) discuss these aspects in detail.

Figure 10.1: A visualisation of the core elements of app platforms and how their behaviour leads to (systemic) risks

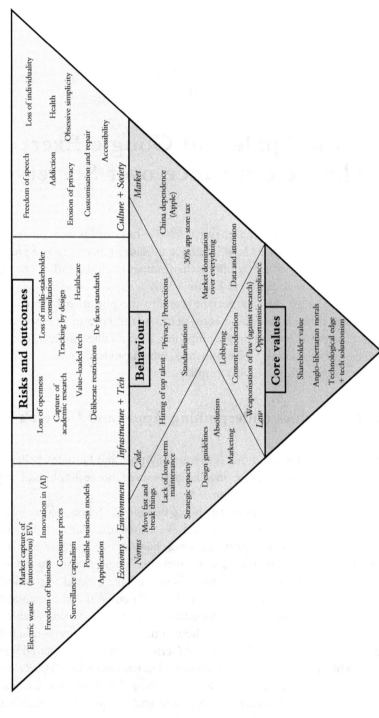

Note: This overview is not meant to be exhaustive, but rather to give a guiding framework to understand Apple and Google's actions in the app economy.

In 2020, Apple issued a public statement titled 'Our Commitment to Human Rights'. In it, the company portrayed itself as an avid defender of human rights in the world. Among other aspects, this document stated that: 'Hand in hand with the privacy of our users is our commitment to freedom of information and expression' (Cook, 2020). Interestingly, this document was issued in response to long-running criticism by its shareholders that alleged that Apple gave in too easily to demands by the Chinese leadership (*Financial Times,* 2020a). After all, most of their products are produced in China, and many are also sold there. This makes China a key market for Apple. Apple's alleged commitment to human rights, arguably, didn't stand the test of time. In 2022, Apple, following civil unrest in China, pushed an update to iOS devices worldwide that made the sharing of information between devices of protesters more difficult (*Bloomberg,* 2022a). This update was pushed worldwide and has thereby impeded the freedom of expression and right to protest of Apple users across the globe. Chapter 6 (on monetisation and content moderation) discusses the intertwinement between Apple and China in detail.

As discussed, for the longest time, both Apple and Google implemented various techniques that helped undermine users' privacy protections, such as advertising and other identifiers. Further, as succinctly pointed out by the UK Competition and Markets Authority, Apple often opportunistically uses privacy and security concerns to extend its control over the app economy and shut out potential competitors (Competition and Markets Authority, 2022b). The ambivalence of Apple regarding privacy was also highlighted in the ongoing lawsuit in the US concerning Google's payments to competitors, such as Apple, to make Google the default search engine on iOS and other platforms. The court case revealed that, for making Google the default search engine in its products, Apple receives 36 per cent of Google's search advertising revenues generated through Apple's Safari browser (Archive et al, 2023). This amounts to about $20 billion per year, almost as much as Apple derives from selling Mac computers per year (Bloomberg, 2024b). However, Google Search famously relies on the widespread tracking of individuals across the web and is thus in conflict with privacy protection online. Chapter 7 (on data protection, privacy and the rule of law) discussed these aspects in detail.

Despite all the claims about human rights, including privacy and freedom of expression, both Apple and Google are still publicly traded companies that are primarily bound to provide value for their shareholders. Indeed, the companies are, by law, obliged to do so.

Putting morals and economic incentives aside, a cornerstone of the tech companies' work is a genuine technological edge. After all, they employ many of the best tech talents worldwide and, through this, have developed a variety of innovations that many of us have come to cherish. With such great knowledge also comes struggles. Those who work in technology are often too easily drawn towards the belief that technology is the solution to everything (tech solutionism). As stated by Tim Cook in Apple's 2020 human rights commitment: 'At Apple, we are optimistic about technology's awesome potential for good' (Cook, 2020). In the context of the COVID-19 pandemic (as discussed in the Introduction), it could be argued that this belief led to false assumptions about the potential of contact-tracing apps, as discussed before.

10.2 Behaviours resulting from core values

These core values, then, translate into certain behaviours. It is helpful to categorise these behaviours into four broad categories: markets, norms, code, and law. These four aspects, as argued by Lawrence Lessig in his book *Code 2.0*, are the key drivers of outcomes (that is, including risks) in digital systems (Lessig, 2006). Along similar lines as Lessig, Christian Fuchs argued that 'social media and the Internet in society deal with three broad issues: the economy, politics and culture' (Fuchs, 2021). Law and code, in Lessig's framework, are the central political sphere of digital platforms (politics); norms, respectively markets, broadly translate to Fuchs' economy, respectively culture.

Regarding markets, there are, for example, Google and Apple's tax on any revenue on the app stores and Apple's dependence on China for its manufacturing and revenue, see Chapter 6. As for law, both companies heavily lobby politicians and arguably weaponise existing laws and technical standards against researchers and competitors (for example, Apple's FairPlay DRM), see Chapter 5. As for code and norms, the two companies play a critical role in standardising apps and cultural production through their app design guidelines (see Chapters 6 and 8. These behaviours show some similarities with other online platforms, but also important differences. While lobbying is common among many online platforms, an intertwinement with China, technical standard-setting and design guidelines play a more limited role for other commonly studied platforms, such as Facebook or Amazon. This underlines that app stores deserve scrutiny in their own right, as performed in this book. It should be stated that this list of behaviours is incomplete. They are illustrated throughout the book.

A crucial behaviour that underlies these practices is how the tech companies, not only Apple and Google, manage to hire much of the top tech talent. Their monopoly rents allow them to pay these talents salaries that are impossible for companies to match, which compete fairly and on the merits, as they should. In particular, this talent is then absent from academia and regulators, who are supposed to hold the companies to account. It is no secret that tech companies have previously hired whole labs from academia, with the aim of furthering their own AI expertise. In addition, even if academics wish to hold the companies to account, they commonly rely on support from the tech companies, for example, to access data (see Section 5.2.4) or to match their technical capabilities.

Never before has the gap between academic and industry salaries been so acute as in the tech sector, at the expense of educating the next generation of AI researchers properly and navigating the current wave of AI innovation.

10.3 Risks and outcomes emerging from the behaviours

In terms of risks and outcomes, some of them are discussed in detail in the chapters of this book. Chapters 6–9 focused on specific risks. Not all risks may pass the bar for a systemic risk in the legal sense of the DSA, but still deserve scrutiny. There are many of them, as shown in Figure 10.1, and this overview is far from complete. To obtain a grasp of these risks and outcomes, it is worthwhile to group them into three categories: economy and environment, infrastructure and technology, and culture and society.

Regarding economy and environment, a common theme across all chapters was how Apple and Google use their dominance in one sector to become dominant in another. Therefore, the two companies hold more data about our day-to-day lives than most other entities. In the world of AI, this is especially important because data is the lifeblood and foundation of AI. As noted in Chapter 3, Apple and Google's dominance in key technologies of the 21st century will likely give them a crucial advantage in deciding the course of AI innovation and becoming market leaders themselves. This will also give them a crucial role in the healthcare sector, which relies ever more on data, tech, and AI. Chapter 9 discussed how smartphone technology increasingly is the basis for innovation in other sectors, even in EVs. Given Trump's re-election and changing norms in Silicon Valley, it is likely that the two companies, besides other tech companies, will increasingly move into the defence sector.

Chapter 6 delved in detail into how Apple and Google decide what business models flourish on the app stores. In particular, the app store tax of 30 per cent was discussed, and how it directly feeds through to consumer prices for products. While Zuboff's surveillance capitalism (see Section 8.2) is part of this, it fails to capture the essence of Apple's business model, which is less focused on data and attention. This, again, underlines that the app economy deserves study in its own right.

Regarding infrastructure and technology, a theme that was shared across various chapters was how Apple and Google design crucial infrastructure for the 21st century. This was demonstrated by how the two companies affected the design and rollout of digital contract-tracing, as discussed in the Introduction. It shows how they have managed to replace, to an extent, established democratic multi-stakeholder decision-making processes with one that serves their own bottom line. The interests of the platforms are often aligned, in which case this is not too much of a concern, but not always.

In the domain of culture and society, we might well lack sufficient scrutiny and discussion the most. Here, technical and non-technical scholarship uniquely come together, with few experts being able to navigate this domain. In response, Chapter 8 embarked on the ambitious mission of teasing apart some of these trends. Admittedly, whole books could be dedicated to these topics, and this book is unable to give a full coverage of them. However, instead of providing end-to-end solutions for all the risks and problems in the app economy, this book foremost strives to encourage the critical reader to think, become curious, and contribute their ideas to addressing some of the looming challenges. The increase in (children's mental) health struggles, discussed in Chapter 8, is just one of many, but might well be the most pressing.

11

How to Respond to Apple and Google's Dominance

This book touched on various facets of the app economy, trying to untangle the centralisation of control with Apple and Google and the resulting societal harms more than previous work. This chapter now turns to potential remedies for these issues. Interestingly, Apple and Google might be obliged to implement some of these remedies, given that they have to implement appropriate mitigation measures against systemic risks emerging from their platforms under the DSA, as highlighted in previous research (Kollnig and Shadbolt, 2023).

11.1 Duty of care, feedback mechanisms, and digital democracy

App store providers commonly argue that they wish to do more to protect users but that this is difficult for them, given that they have limited resources and are faced with a large ecosystem of millions of apps. However, this argument is hardly convincing, given that Google and Apple derive billions in revenue from the app ecosystems every year. At the same time, we're seeing an unprecedented increase in the prevalence of mental health issues, particularly among the young. This increase has very accurately coincided with the release of smartphones to the world. While it is difficult to prove causation, and it is unlikely that smartphones are the only reason for this, they probably have played a role.

In light of this, it is surprising that apps' use of problematic design elements plays little role in the app review processes of either Apple or Google. They never hesitate to emphasise the security of their app ecosystems (Competition and Markets Authority, 2022b), but ostensibly fail at moving beyond cybersecurity towards including health and personal autonomy in their conception of security. Judging what is harmful in digital devices and what isn't is challenging. Thousands of pages have been written about this. However, a precise definition is not always necessary to keep users safer.

Moving forward, it is important to recognise the duty of app store providers to care more strongly. In common law systems, the duty of care has a particular meaning that may be inappropriate for this specific case. Instead, what is important to underline is that store providers should err strongly on the side of caution and that of the users, especially in case of doubt about whether some elements of an app are harmful, as discussed in Chapter 8. The DSA already goes some way in these directions, but has an overly broad focus on systemic risks and mainly restricts itself to content moderation on social media. This makes it necessary to consider more targeted interventions and obligations in the app economy. Without this, it is unlikely that we will meaningfully ensure the rule of law in the app economy and that applicable laws are respected and followed.

Towards these aims, it will be necessary for app stores to establish better feedback and complaints mechanisms for users. As it stands, only minimal contact points exist at the app stores. For users who experience significant digital harm and other issues, there should be easy means to bring this up with Apple and Google, and have their concerns investigated swiftly and diligently.

This idea could even be extended so that users can petition specific changes, which must be implemented, provided a quorum is reached. This would not be unprecedented. In the early days of Facebook, the platform needed permission from its users to roll out policy changes. Further, it is common for tech companies to maintain public repositories where users can vote on potential changes. However, whether these will be implemented is usually up to the tech company in question.

The suggestion of involving users more actively in platform governance is rooted in that of Yale professor Hélène Landemore, who is a strong advocate of rethinking modern-day democracy away from party politics towards something closer to what Greek city-states (polis) used to have in ancient times. In her work, she advocates for ideas like lottocracy (where representatives are chosen at random), liquid democracy (where citizens can delegate their vote on specific issues to more knowledgeable individuals), and citizen assemblies (where everyday citizens convene, discuss, and decide). These ideas are made particularly palpable in her essay 'Open democracy and digital technologies' (Landemore, 2021). Here, Landemore tries to take a leap into the near future and anticipate what this may look like. She imagines citizens discussing and deciding on important societal issues on a website called 'Citizenbook', previously called Facebook, until Mark Zuckerberg turned it into a non-profit organisation. Today, Facebook may appear as a soulless place full of cat videos and advertising. However, once upon a time, it was a place that wished to grow, was much less monetised, and where people genuinely came together to discuss in good faith. There appears to be no reason why such a platform could not be realised again if its (financial) incentives were closely aligned with those of its users. A non-profit organisation, as considered later in this chapter for the app economy (see Section 11.5), might be a good breeding ground for this.

Landemore's ideas are provocative precisely because they put trust in everyday citizens rather than deciding over their heads and believing that many of them are stupid or do not care, which is what citizens often feel like with career politicians. They might also have a place in tech governance. They might be particularly suitable for it because there is also an existing technological foundation that can serve as a testing ground for rolling out new approaches to democracy in other parts of society.

11.2 A right to repair for apps, and our entire surroundings

Beyond a duty of care, a right to repair harmful apps could provide further protection for end users.

What if, instead of being provided with limited choice of how apps look and function, users were given the ability to reconfigure and reshape the essential features of apps, an ability to repair for apps, to make them more suitable to their needs, including the possibility of removing elements that are hostile, manipulative, or harmful to them?

Such capability could empower users both directly, by helping them improve their apps immediately, and indirectly, by exerting pressure on app developers to address their concerns. Beyond eliminating user-hostile app elements, this 'superpower' could be beneficial to improving accessibility and realising more inclusive design, by fixing apps that make incorrect assumptions about their users or their needs, such as those documented previously in fertility and fitness trackers.

Such a capability is something that was developed in work between me, Siddhartha Datta and others from the University of Oxford. First, a method was developed through which distracting and annoying parts can easily be removed from apps (Kollnig et al, 2021; Kollnig et al, 2023). This makes it possible, for example, to remove unwanted ads from apps in the same way that ad blockers allow this in desktop browsers. Mobile apps currently do not include this functionality, not because it isn't technically feasible, but because, among other things, Google relies on advertising revenue and because Apple sees user customisation as the ultimate threat to its design philosophy of simplicity (see Chapter 8).

Moving forward, the idea of removing such elements was combined with the latest advances in machine learning and AI, for instance, few-shot learning (Datta et al, 2022b; 2022a). A system was built that allows users to take screenshots of annoying elements in their digital environments and then let them, without the need for any programming skills, hide those annoying elements in the future. This system was developed for all common device types, including Android, iOS, Windows, and Linux.

Lastly, the same system in the real world, with the help of VR glasses (Datta, 2022). Again, the system allows users to note things they do not wish to see and consequently hide them from their experienced physical reality. This could, for example, include billboard ads that one doesn't want to see. An ad blocker for the real world may not be far off and could be one of the most valuable applications of VR technologies in the real world, minimising undesired noise and distractions in a capitalistic world.

However, like most technology that aims to 'empower', what can be used for good can also be used for harm; modifications to apps could bring about any number of unwanted harms to end users, such as weakening app security or adding malicious code that perpetuates criminal activity or steals from users. Therefore, more work is needed.

11.3 Agile, technology-specific regulation

Compliance with applicable laws, including those relating to privacy and data protection, is widely absent in the app economy, leading to (systemic) risks in the app economy. There are at least two issues at the heart of this.

First, the resources of the responsible authorities are tight. In their enforcement actions, they usually focus on a few cases per year and only on the largest players. The smaller players do not have to fear consequences for non-compliance. This is further held back by the fact that authorities commonly lack sufficient technical expertise, given that authorities traditionally didn't require such expertise. The targets of enforcement are also often based outside the immediate jurisdiction of the authority, for example, in India, making enforcement even more difficult. This makes it even more critical to bring successful enforcement action.

This makes it important to emphasise the app stores' role in enforcement and their duty to care to ensure the rule of law in the app economy (see Section 11.1). After all, they span borders and have leading technical expertise.

Second, laws are often written in a technology-neutral way. This is done to ensure that laws keep up with the rapid changes in technology. But it doesn't work. Technology keeps changing fast, and often just ignores the principles, because interpreting them takes time. This makes enforcement extremely hard in practice. When, for example, is consent really 'informed' and 'freely given', as is required under the GDPR? No one really knows, and it's difficult to translate such legal norms directly into code.

Azeem Azhar describes these challenges in his book *Exponential: How Accelerating Technology is Leaving us Behind and What to do About It* (Azhar, 2021). He traces how different cutting edge technologies have developed over time and have been improving at an exponential rate. A key element of this is the learning rate. This describes how, for every doubling of production of solar panels, for example, the cost of production falls by a certain percentage. In the case of solar panels, the learning rate has consistently been about 20 per cent, which has made the installation of solar the most efficient form of energy production, even exceeding that of coal or nuclear. During the COVID-19 pandemic, the effect of exponential development was most visible when a few infections turned into millions within mere days.

Meanwhile, Azhar argues that traditional institutions operate at a linear speed, making it almost impossible for them to keep pace. There are good reasons why institutions, at least in democratic countries, only move at a limited speed. This serves as a safeguard to prevent the abuse of power. It also has the effect that those with power in other domains of society might end up making their own rules according to their own pace and liking. We commonly see this in digital platforms, including app stores. Crucially, this is not necessarily a bad thing. After all, the interests of society and platform providers have some alignment; otherwise, these products would not be used. What is important, however, is to have checks and balances in place for when interests collide and may cause societal risks, such as those highlighted in this book.

This makes it important to improve the translation from law to code and enforce legal safeguards in practice.

To improve the translation from law into tech, a radically new approach to tech regulation is necessary, as argued in Kollnig (2023). The current approach has failed because it doesn't scale and doesn't adequately protect citizens. Instead of being technology-neutral (like the GDPR), regulation must move more quickly than it currently does and more closely track the steps of technology. After all, the saying goes that the law always follows technology. However, this doesn't mean that there must be a large gap between the two. The aim should be to narrow this gap as far as possible through an agile approach to regulation, similar to the agile approach to software engineering that is commonly used. Importantly, this idea goes beyond the 'clear, reliable and actionable technical standards' argued for in Kollnig (2023). Instead, a new approach to tech regulation will be outlined here.

After all, if software companies can change their code within minutes in response to regulatory and other stimuli, then why should law and policy makers not be able to do the same by using and changing code that encapsulates the law?

If one looks at the authorities of the digital space, it stands out that few of them actually provide any code. This can easily be verified by trying to find the GitHub pages of the relevant authorities. In the field of data protection, the EU lead authority, the European Data Protection Board, has a Git account,[1] but only a single public repository that focuses on evidence collection from websites. Many other authorities do not share any code publicly or have any repositories or Git accounts. This shows that the responsible authorities speak a fundamentally different language from those who write code.

To change that, a first important step would be to share more concrete details on how to comply with certain key provisions of relevant laws. While there are hundreds of laws that any app must comply with at any time, certain legal obligations are surely more important than others and pose more risks if not complied with. This is also acknowledged in new EU laws, like the AI Act, that embrace a risk-based (but still relatively technology-neutral) approach to compliance. There seems to be broad agreement that how apps request consent from users and whether apps send sensitive data to a third-party company are some of the aspects that app providers should be particularly careful about. This could be a start.

Identifying key provisions would also provide more explicit guidance to app stores on what they need to check in their app review process. Right now, the review guidelines of the app stores merely contain blanket statements on the fact that compliance with all applicable laws is necessary, but legal compliance is rarely explicitly assessed. If key provisions of laws are not enforced adequately within the app stores, then this could indicate negligence on the part of the app store provider, lead to systemic risks, and ultimately provide grounds for fines under the DSA. The aim here would be to give app store providers a more explicit role in ensuring compliance with legal principles and the rule of law. This aligns with the idea of a duty of care and the DSA's aim of holding platforms to account for systemic risks in their app ecosystems.

In the specific case of consent, the details could include sample code (or an equivalent) on how such is requested and visualised to the end user. This sample code could, in particular, tie in with other existing standards that make requesting consent less burdensome for end users. For example, in California, the Global Privacy Control provides a system-wide opt-out from the sale of user data (Zimmeck et al, 2024). However, this standard (or an equivalent) has, so far, not been implemented on mobile or in the EU, due to a lack of support from the responsible stakeholders. On iOS, as discussed in Section 7.3.4, there is the App Tracking Transparency framework (Kollnig et al, 2022b), but it has not had any support from responsible authorities so far.

Importantly, it doesn't always have to be sample code that is the most appropriate form. Depending on the legal objective at hand, there could be other forms that allow better translation into code than traditional legal text, especially since a range of different programming languages and paradigms exist. There are, for example, concrete software requirements or visualisations, both of which should be used more in the legislative process for IT. Other times, Delegated Acts that can be adopted and iterated fast, like those envisioned for DSA Article 40 (see Section 5.3), might be more suitable. The experience of the DSA, however, shows that even supposedly fast-moving Delegated Acts could be too slow-moving and suffer from a large gap between tech and law.

Beyond the concrete way through which regulation is communicated, such as sample code, political support is crucial to ensure rigorous standards are followed. The example of the Global Privacy Control in California is a case in point. It already gives Californians a legally binding way to communicate their data collection preferences to platforms. However, this standard is not implemented inside mobile operating systems and many browsers. This renders the standard out of reach for many consumers and data collection events, such as data collection in mobile apps. In response, the California parliament passed a law that would have forced Apple, Google, and other companies to integrate an explicit and legally binding setting to reduce data collection in their browsers and mobile operating systems. However, after intense lobbying by the tech companies and others, California Governor Gavin Newsom chose to exercise his veto right and stop the law. While Android (and iOS) offer some data controls, these come with serious limitations, as found in recent research. Specifically, Android has integrated an opt-out from tracking for over a decade. However, enabling this setting doesn't make any difference to apps' sharing and collection of data (Zimmeck et al, 2024).

An example of what such code for compliance could look like has been created by the author. The tool 'auto-app-consent' is available freely on open source, and, by adding just three lines of code, configures data sharing with third-party companies in an app in a manner that is likely legally compliant and sets a high bar for consent. The tool is shown in action in Figure 11.1. It took a few days to build this tool, which underlines that it should be possible for authorities to build something similar easily and for companies to comply relatively easily (Kollnig and Dewitte, 2023). Even though laws like the GDPR might be principle-based, compliance with them is possible and sometimes not as difficult as commonly thought. Instead, the argument that compliance is allegedly 'hard' is often used to dodge legal standards. For those actors that operate in good faith, compliance is possible but might sometimes be resource-intensive. Many other actors do not wish to comply because they do not want to collect less data and think about alternative strategies to run a lucrative business. Both would be helped by being more explicit about how compliance is accomplished and demonstrated.

Using such premade code would, at least at first, not be mandatory. However, app providers would have to argue in their submission to the app stores whether they request consent inside the app, and if they do so, why they do not do it officially and why the custom implementation is still equivalent.

Figure 11.1: My auto-app-consent tool

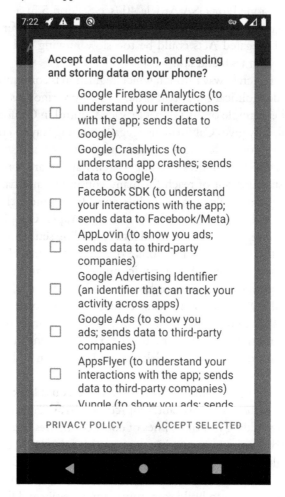

If the app review finds that the implementation is not equivalent, the app would not be allowed to be published on the store. This would, conceptually, take a similar approach to the EU Artificial Intelligence Act, which works with standards. However, the Artificial Intelligence Act has a complex standards verification framework that is unlikely to scale across the vastness of the app economy. Notably, changing the existing legal framework would be unnecessary to develop and distribute sample code, thereby establishing a baseline. Developers would still have an incentive to follow these examples because it speeds up development time and promises more legal certainty.

Premade code would also help the measurability of compliance and enforcement because the code could request additional information from the developer, such as an explanation of why a particularly sensitive information type is requested, or directly run additional analyses on an app's code in order to, for example, verify an app's use of sensitive information. This approach is already used on iOS to handle sensitive in-app permissions, like calendar or camera access. Before deployment, every app must give a textual justification for why this specific type of sensitive data is requested. This textual explanation is then shown by the operating system to the user when the app first wants to access this sensitive data, putting users in charge of whether they agree to this data collection.

Lastly, it should be noted that information disclosures and choice mechanisms have failed (Solove, 2012; Bietti, 2020). Designing better consent pop-ups or information disclosures should, therefore, not be the aim of authorities. Rather, building means for better measurability could be a first step.

11.4 Effective platform data access

Chapter 4 surveyed the legal framework for app platforms. This chapter found that limited explicit legal obligations exist for app stores. This observation does not mean we need a new legal framework in response. What is necessary, however, is to have reliable data available for researchers and authorities so that they can monitor more regularly and rigorously whether apps, and their underlying platforms, uphold user protections. The DSA takes a first step. However, as described in Chapter 5, which briefly introduced the analysis of apps on the app stores, including the DSA, this still falls short.

A critical element of ensuring the success of the DSA data access rules will be that the authorities ensure that platforms provide researchers with requested data fully, fairly, and expediently. In both the cases of Apple and Google, this is already not always the case. As discussed in Section 5.3, under the DSA's obligations to provide publicly accessible platform data to researchers, Apple provides some data but refuses to provide app packages to researchers, counterintuitively claiming that they are not public data. Google doesn't provide any data or help at all to researchers. These challenges will likely become more acute as researchers will also be able to request non-public data. In this case, it will be nearly impossible for researchers to assess whether data was provided fully, given the non-public nature of that data.

Beyond mere data access, platforms could be obliged to provide more specific data on how they ensure compliance on their app stores. If premade code is used (as suggested in the previous section), this would be particularly easy by merely making accessible details on how the app developers implement these. Roşca (2024) supports this view.

Even if premade code is not used, one pertinent example of sharing compliance data is data flows within mobile apps. As part of the app review process, Apple and Google already use a range of techniques to understand apps' behaviour, including how they use user data. Some of the most commonly used of these techniques are sandbox testing and flow analysis. In the case of sandbox testing, apps are installed and run in an automated manner, on a testing phone and their behaviour is documented and assessed. This also routinely monitors apps' network traffic, including what types of data are sent to what companies. In the case of flow analysis, without ever running the app, the flow of data from critical sources (for example, phone contacts, the GPS sensor, and the phone number) to critical sinks (for example, internet communications and the SD card) is logged. Again, this analysis may easily help uncover what data is sent where.

Additionally, flow analysis can provide this data on a library level, thereby giving insights into the behaviour of third-party libraries that are commonly used for user tracking. The results of this analysis are usually not shared, but could be very helpful for relevant stakeholders. These results also likely exist in Apple and Google, and even if they don't, they would be very easy to generate for them.

It remains unclear if the DSA mandates access to platform data that the platform could easily generate but is not yet readily available.

As a result of these efforts, researchers and authorities should, ideally, be able to monitor the full breadth of platforms and get access to relevant information about compliance, at least as it pertains to key provisions for compliance.

11.5 Divestment into an independent entity

Suppose we do not manage to address the issues within the app economy and untangle Google and Apple's interests from those of users. In that case, we may have to take a more radical step: divestment of the infrastructure underpinning the app economy into an independent entity.

Chapter 6 covered the financial and monetary aspects of app platforms. This chapter underlined how Apple and Google design their ecosystems to serve their financial bottom line. This was also highlighted in Chapter 7, which examined data protection and privacy challenges. In response, it might be worthwhile to consider ways to reduce conflicts of interest. One option might be divestment into an independent organisation. This might sound like a radical step, but it is something that is already seriously considered.

Following a lawsuit led by the US government, Google was found to operate an illegal monopoly in online search (see Section 4.4.2). This might hardly be surprising. After all, we refer to searching for information online as 'Googling'. What is interesting, however, is to reflect on the exact role that Android plays in maintaining Google's monopoly. As highlighted in the lawsuit, one of the key strategies that Google uses to ensure the dominance of its search product is to control the distribution channels of search. This means that: (1) Google pays competitors to be set as the default search, including in Apple products and the Firefox browser; and (2) Google maintains its search distribution channels, such as Chrome and Android. This way, Google ensures that virtually no competitors can easily replace it.

However, it goes further than that. Google's business model is principally rooted in the collection of data to show users ads. Controlling Android (and Chrome) gives Google an enormous competitive advantage in the advertising market, including in the advertising market for search ads and other ads, such as those shown inside apps or on websites. Google is the most dominant company across all these different ad categories. This is likely extremely bad for consumers because it allows Google to charge advertisers more for showing ads, which, in turn, makes products that are advertised more costly. It also likely prevents innovations in various markets, including those for ads and search, since Google has limited incentive to change a running, and highly lucrative, system. Google's access to data and prominence in online services also give the company a significant competitive advantage in other digital services, including developing the latest AI products.

As a result, the US government now proposes that the divestment of Android from Google should be considered (Reuters, 2024d). The case for this was neatly outlined by many before, notably by Morton et al (2024). Moreover, the US government argues for the immediate sale of Chrome because it poses similar problems but is less tightly integrated into Google's overall business and is, therefore, much easier to sell without negative effects on the company's innovativeness. The case to sell Chrome was first made in detail by the author in Munir et al (2024).

Meanwhile, Apple also enjoys significant competitive advantages by controlling a major part of the supply chain, both in software and hardware, in the iOS ecosystem. Importantly, having a competitive advantage is not illegal per se. What may be unlawful, however, is the abuse of a dominant position in the market. Here, Apple is also subject to a flurry of ongoing lawsuits, including those relating to its 30 per cent commission, its limitations on alternative browsers and the distribution of cloud gaming providers and alternative app stores, and the unequal treatment of competitors in Apple's privacy rules. Power is commonly thought to corrupt those who hold it. And in comparison, Apple seems to hold more power in its ecosystem than Google does. This is, for example, evidenced by the fact that Apple doesn't need to pay its competitors billions of US dollars every year to maintain its dominance. In light of this, divestment of the iOS ecosystem might also be worthwhile to consider, stimulating competition in the mobile app economy.

A divestment of iOS, for example, could create an incentive to integrate a compatibility layer for Android apps into the iOS ecosystem (and vice versa). This would allow the direct operation of Android apps on iOS. The development of this would be relatively straightforward because Android and iOS are Linux-compatible (UNIX-compatible, to be precise) and run technically similar operating systems. Such compatibility layers have already been created for BlackBerry, Windows Phone (Project Astoria), and the Chrome Operating System. Cross compatibility between iOS and Android would significantly reduce app development costs because only one code base would have to be maintained. Currently, companies usually develop two separate apps, one for Android and one for iOS.

One might argue that any divestment would be unfair to the great level of innovation that was produced by private companies, foremost Apple and Google. However, this leaves out that the taxpayer made great upfront investments to get smartphones started. A good account of this is provided in *The Entrepreneurial State* (Mazzucato, 2018). In particular, she traces the history of the components of the iPhone. She points out that many of its key components, including the GPS, the internet, the lithium-ion battery, and the multitouch screen, all started as developments for the US military.

11.6 Increasing sustainability and security

The need for divestment might be especially acute as app technology moves into new areas, as Chapter 9 showed, such as EVs and IoT devices. This is also true for the adoption of AI technologies, as highlighted in Chapter 3: Apple and Google have an unprecedented concentration of control in IT technologies and will be able to (co)decide about winners and losers in consumer AI. This divestment could ultimately help to create genuine competition between iOS and Android by making all operating systems compatible with both systems.

Working towards more openness in Android and iOS might also bring some hope for ensuring a longer lifetime of devices and thereby alleviate sustainability concerns attached to them, as Chapter 9 showed. After all, many modern Windows computers can run software dating back to the 1980s. Meanwhile, many smartphones are only compatible with the software from the past few years.

More generally, the smartphone economy, as driven by Apple and Google, has established a new paradigm for software development that allows for faster cycles of innovation and development but is also prone to obsolescence. To mitigate a loss of resources, it is necessary to have much richer documentation obligations (both as they pertain to hardware and software), support for independent maintenance (including parts and manuals), and easy-to-use abilities for the independent inspection of smart devices. Android users should have the option to use an unmodified version of the operating system, which would decrease the occurrence of software flaws and increase long-term maintainability. Google Treble and Generic

System Image already provide a foundation upon which app developers can receive the latest Android version for their phones without the intervention of phone manufacturers; this should be extended to end-users, not just app developers. The supply of security updates should last longer than 2 years and be communicated at the point of sale. Lastly, the locking of bootloaders by manufacturers should be limited. It makes security research much more difficult and prevents end users from installing more secure or more up-to-date versions of Android. The use of Google's SafetyNet, which prevents the installation of modified versions of Android, should be restricted because it hinders such community efforts and app security research.

Concluding Thoughts: Building App Infrastructure to Withstand Geopolitics

App infrastructure plays a special role in the platform economy. It is an all-purpose tool, rather than one built for a specific purpose like social media. In the past, when there was shared infrastructure across the globe, it was usually subject to stringent international treaties and cooperation. This, at least, was true in the tech space, with the Internet and the World Wide Web having been traditionally governed by multi-stakeholder committees rather than a single private company. In the app economy, there is none of that.

Admittedly, the digital economy is fast-moving. Some of the thoughts and observations in this book may become outdated quickly. And yet, the question of how to deal with key digital infrastructure that is in the hands of a few private companies will not go away, especially in times of geopolitical crisis. Indeed, there is reason to believe that these challenges will become more acute as these companies become dominant in new sectors, such as AI, healthcare and defence, thereby cementing their dominance for years to come. A historical understanding of that technology and of how to merge technical and legal considerations behind it, as attempted in this book, will remain essential for any consideration of what to do in response.

From a non-US perspective, we must ask ourselves to what extent we wish to tolerate the trajectory and pace of innovation in tech being primarily set in the US. As discussed in this book, the EU and other jurisdictions have been trying to respond to this, but their efforts have had a limited effect on the status quo. The only nation that can match the size and determination of the US is China. It is important to note that China has paid a price for being less integrated with technology and ideas outside the country, particularly those from the US. Yet, maybe, this was worth it. Outside China, countries remain wholly dependent on US technology in almost every single element of the technology stack. In Europe, this is especially acute in the AI space, where it lacks much of the necessary knowledge in the sourcing of raw materials, chip production, computing clusters, and top talent. None of this will change unless one is willing to bear and sustain the immense costs of decoupling.

The lack of industrial expertise is met, in many places around the world, with a lack of administrative expertise. For example, the EU desperately tries to hire talent in tech but tends to offer them relatively low pay and fixed-term contracts. A substantial commitment is necessary to establish attractive working conditions for tech talent outside big tech. This does not necessarily mean a financial commitment matching the pay of the industry, but rather the creation of a stimulating environment. A highly bureaucratic apparatus like that of Brussels is unattractive for many graduates who, from their work, are used to achieving quick results in an iterative manner by means of writing code. It truly can be an addictive undertaking.

Moving forward, creating a stronger shared voice regarding what the tech ecosystem should look like is important. These voices, currently, are way too scattered and unorganised. Collective action is especially difficult, given the global reach of a few large tech companies. Landemore's ideas (see Section 11.1) could be a good start, but tailoring them to the governance of digital platforms requires more work. Bluesky, allowing for alternative protocols and Anthropic being run as a public benefit company, also shows some innovation in terms of building better and more democratic technical infrastructure. Nevertheless, the idea of hearing, trusting, and enabling the individual, that is, the user and subject of technology, seems to be a forgotten art in dire need of reinvigoration. Therefore, we should strive to ensure that the big decisions concerning online platforms regarding the appropriate balance of fundamental rights, for example, during the COVID-19 pandemic, as described in the Introduction, are made through the appropriate bodies free of conflicts of interest and for the public benefit.

These debates are some of the most pressing of our times, and are constantly evolving. They will be covered in even more detail in future publications. If you, as a reader, have any ideas you wish to share on this or other topics, then please do not hesitate to reach out at book@trackercontrol.org.

Notes

Chapter 4

[1] These browser engines are the 'heart' of web browsers. They implement how the device interacts with websites and turn the computer code underlying those websites into graphical content for end-users. Every web browser, such as Google Chrome or Mozilla Firefox, integrates a browser engine. Browsers only play the role of providing additional features and visualisation, such as allowing end-users to switch between different browser windows or tabs.

Chapter 5

[1] Available at: https://platformcontrol.org
[2] Available at: https://play.google.com/store/apps/details?id=com.spotify.music
[3] Available at: https://github.com/TrackerControl/platformcontrol-ios-downloader
[4] Available at: https://exodus-privacy.eu/en/
[5] Available at: https://ios.trackercontrol.org
[6] Available at: https://github.com/MobSF/Mobile-Security-Framework-MobSF

Chapter 7

[1] For example, Google argues that 'pseudonymous cookie IDs', 'pseudonymous advertising IDs', 'IP addresses', and 'other pseudonymous end user identifiers' do not fall under its own definition of 'Personally Identifiable Information' (PII); Available at: https://support.google.com/analytics/answer/7686480?hl=en

Chapter 8

[1] According to the World Inequality Database, everyone earning above €109,078 falls within that category (last checked 27 July 2023).

Chapter 11

[1] Available at: https://code.europa.eu/edpb/

References

9to5Google (2022) 'Android removes much of Fuchsia-related code as Starnix project progresses', 9to5Google, [online] nd, Available from: https://9to5google.com/2022/07/15/android-removes-fuchsia-code-starnix/ [Accessed 3 September 2024].

9to5Mac (2020a) 'Apple rebuffs Facebook criticism, says iOS anti-tracking features are about 'standing up for our users', 9to5Mac, [online] nd, Available from: https://9to5mac.com/2020/12/16/apple-facebook-app-tracking-transparency/ [Accessed 23 February 2023].

9to5Mac (2020b) 'Facebook attacks Apple in full-page newspaper ads over ad-tracking', 9to5Mac, [online] nd, Available from: https://9to5mac.com/2020/12/16/facebook-attacks-apple/ [Accessed 23 February 2023].

9to5Mac (2021) 'Apple versus Facebook on ad-tracking: Harvard sides with Apple', 9to5Mac, [online] nd, Available from: https://9to5mac.com/2021/02/05/Epic-versus-facebook-harvard/ [Accessed 23 February 2023].

42matters (2023) 'Apple App Store Statistics and Trends 2023', 42matters, [online] nd, Available from: https://42matters.com/ios-apple-app-store-statistics-and-trends [Accessed 2 February 2023].

ABC (2021) 'Police access SafeWA app data for murder investigation, prompting urgent law change', ABC News, [online] nd, Available from: https://www.abc.net.au/news/2021-06-15/safewa-app-sparks-urgent-law-change-after-police-access-data/100201340 [Accessed 4 May 2025].

Acquisti, A., Taylor, C. and Wagman, L. (2016) 'The economics of privacy', *Journal of Economic Literature*, 18(2): 64.

Agarwal, Y. and Hall, M. (2013) 'ProtectMyPrivacy: Detecting and mitigating privacy leaks on iOS devices using crowdsourcing', in Proceedings of the 11th Annual International Conference on Mobile Systems, Applications, and Services. (MobiSys '13). ACM Press, p 97.

Ajunwa, I. and Greene, D. (2019) 'Platforms at work: Automated hiring platforms and other new intermediaries in the organization of work', in S.P. Vallas and A. Kovalainen (eds) *Research in the Sociology of Work*. Emerald Publishing Limited, pp 61–91.

AlgorithmWatch (2021) 'Digital contact tracing apps: Do they actually work? A review of early evidence', AlgorithmWatch, [online] nd, Available from: https://algorithmwatch.org/en/analysis-digital-contact-tracing-apps-2021/ [Accessed 21 November 2022].

Alphabet (2024) 'Form 10-K', [online] Available from: https://www.sec.gov/Archives/edgar/data/1652044/000165204425000014/goog-20241231.htm [Accessed 22 August 2025].

Amnesty International (2020) 'Norway halts COVID-19 contact tracing app a major win for privacy', Amnesty International, [online] Available from: https://www.amnesty.org/en/latest/news/2020/06/norway-covid19-contact-tracing-app-privacy-win/ [Accessed 4 May 2025].

Android Authority (2016) 'Runkeeper is secretly tracking you around the clock and sending your data to advertisers', Android Authority, [online] Available from: https://www.androidauthority.com/runkeeper-user-location-tracking-data-advertisers-692346/ [Accessed 11 August 2023].

Appel, G., Libia, B., Muller, E., and Shachar, R. (2020) 'On the monetization of mobile apps', *International Journal of Research in Marketing*, 37(1): 93–107.

Apple (2024a) 'Core technology fee – support' Apple Developer, [online] Available from: https://developer.apple.com/support/core-technology-fee/ [Accessed 9 May 2024].

Apple (2024b) 'Apple advertising & Privacy', Apple Legal, [online] Available from: https://www.apple.com/legal/privacy/data/en/apple-advertising/ [Accessed 29 December 2024].

Apple (2024c) '10-K Filing', Available from: https://www.sec.gov/Archives/edgar/data/320193/000032019324000123/aapl-20240928.htm [Accessed 22 August 2025].

New York Post (2023) 'Google witness accidentally reveals company pays Apple 36% of search ad revenue', Available from: https://nypost.com/2023/11/13/business/google-witness-accidentally-reveals-company-pays-apple-36-of-search-ad-revenue/ [Accessed 7 May 2024].

Ars Technica (2020) 'Google kills Android Things, its IoT OS, in January', Ars Technica. [online] nd, Available from: https://arstechnica.com/gadgets/2020/12/google-kills-android-things-its-iot-os-in-january/ [Accessed 3 September 2024].

Ars Technica (2022) 'Google's Fuchsia OS is taking over smart displays, now on its second device', Ars Technica, [online] Available from: https://arstechnica.com/gadgets/2022/08/googles-fuchsia-os-lands-on-its-second-device-the-nest-hub-max/ [Accessed 3 September 2024].

Azhar, A. (2021) *Exponential: How Accelerating Technology is Leaving us Behind and What to Do About It.* Random House Business.

BBC (2023) 'Google sends a third of Safari ad revenue to Apple', [online] Available from: https://www.bbc.com/news/business-67417987 [Accessed 2 August 2024].

Benjamin, R. (2019) *Race After Technology: Abolitionist Tools for the New Jim Code*. Polity Press.

Bietti, E. (2020) 'Consent as a free pass: Platform power and the limits of the informational turn', *Pace Law Review*, 40(1): 60.

Binns, R., Zhao, J., Kleek, M. and Shadbolt, N. (2018a) 'Measuring third-party tracker power across web and mobile', *ACM Transactions on Internet Technology*, 18(4): 1–22.

Binns, R., Lyngs, Van Kleek, M., Zhao, J., Libert, T. and Shadbolt, M. (2018) 'Third party tracking in the mobile ecosystem', in Proceedings of the 10th ACM Conference on Web Science. 27–30 May. ACM Press, pp 23–31.

Binns, R. and Bietti, E. (2020) 'Dissolving privacy, one merger at a time: Competition, data and third party tracking', *Computer Law & Security Review*, 36.

Bloomberg (2022a) 'Apple limits iPhone file-sharing tool used for protests in China', Bloomberg.com, [online] 10 November, Available from: https://www.bloomberg.com/news/articles/2022-11-10/apple-limits-iphone-file-sharing-tool-used-for-protests-in-china [Accessed 9 July 2024].

Bloomberg (2022b) 'Google, Apple rivals to launch ad campaign for bill against big tech', Bloomberg.com, [online] 14 November, Available from: https://www.bloomberg.com/news/articles/2022-11-14/google-apple-rivals-launch-ad-campaign-for-anti-big-tech-bill [Accessed 8 May 2024].

Bloomberg (2023) 'China's iPhone ban accelerates across government and state firms', Bloomberg.com, [online] 15 December, Available from: https://www.bloomberg.com/news/articles/2023-12-15/china-s-apple-iphone-ban-accelerates-across-state-firms-government [Accessed 2 August 2024].

Bloomberg (2024a) 'Apple to wind down electric car effort after decade-long odyssey', Bloomberg.com, [online] 27 February, Available from: https://www.bloomberg.com/news/articles/2024-02-27/apple-cancels-work-on-electric-car-shifts-team-to-generative-ai [Accessed 3 September 2024].

Bloomberg (2024b) 'Google's payments to Apple reached $20 billion in 2022, antitrust court documents show', Bloomberg.com, [online] 1 May, Available from: https://www.bloomberg.com/news/articles/2024-05-01/google-s-payments-to-apple-reached-20-billion-in-2022-cue-says [Accessed 7 May 2024].

BroadbandSearch (2023) 'Mobile vs. desktop internet usage (latest 2023 data)', BroadbandSearch.net, [online] nd, Available from: https://www.broadbandsearch.net/blog/mobile-desktop-internet-usage-statistics [Accessed 9 February 2023].

Business Insider (2009) 'Why Apple considered buying AdMob', Business Insider, [online] nd, Available from: https://www.businessinsider.com/why-apple-considered-buying-admob-2009-11 [Accessed 23 February 2023].

Business Insider (2010) 'Why Apple bought Quattro Wireless and is getting into advertising, Business Insider, [online] nd, Available from: https://www.businessinsider.com/why-apple-bought-quattro-wireless-and-is-getting-into-mobile-advertising-2010-1 [Accessed 23 February 2023].

Business Insider (2016) 'Traffic fatalities in the US have been mostly plummeting for decades', Business Insider, [online] nd, Available from: https://www.businessinsider.com/traffic-fatalities-historical-trend-us-2016-4 [Accessed 13 July 2023].

Business of Apps (2021) 'App Data Report 2023', Business of Apps, [online] nd, Available from: https://www.businessofapps.com/data/report-app-data/ [Accessed 8 February 2023].

CBS (2022) 'Tesla won't roll out new models in 2022 because of chip shortages', [online] nd, Available from: https://www.cbsnews.com/news/chip-shortage-delays-tesla-cybertruck-new-models-2022/ [Accessed 13 July 2023].

CEPRO (2024) 'Which Smart TV operating systems are the most popular?' CEPRO, [online] nd, Available from: https://www.cepro.com/audio-video/displays/which-smart-tv-operating-systems-are-the-most-popular/ [Accessed 1 January 2025].

Chen, K., Wang, X., Chen, Y., Wang, P., Lee, Y., Wang, X. et al (2016) 'Following Devil's footprints: Cross-platform analysis of potentially harmful libraries on Android and iOS', in 2016 IEEE Symposium on Security and Privacy (SP). 23–26 May. IEEE, pp 357–76.

Claburn, T. (2022) 'Google Play rule change disallows ad-blocking VPN apps', Available from: https://www.theregister.com/2022/08/30/google_play_vpn_rules_changed/ [Accessed 10 February 2023].

CNBC (2020) 'How a handful of Apple and Google employees came together to help health officials trace coronavirus', CNBC, [online] nd, Available from: https://www.cnbc.com/2020/04/28/apple-iphone-contact-tracing-how-it-came-together.html [Accessed 2 February 2023].

CNBC (2022) 'Apple shares dip after company warns of a possible $8 billion hit from supply constraints', CNBC, [online] nd, Available from: https://www.cnbc.com/2022/04/28/apple-aapl-earnings-q2-2022.html [Accessed 26 March 2023].

CNET (2010) 'Steve Jobs: If you want porn, get an Android', CNET, [online] nd, Available from: https://www.cnet.com/culture/steve-jobs-if-you-want-porn-get-an-android/ [Accessed 11 February 2023].

CNET (2012) 'How to control your privacy settings on iOS 6', CNET, [online] nd, Available from: https://www.cnet.com/culture/how-to-control-your-privacy-settings-on-ios-6/ [Accessed 23 February 2023].

CNN (2024) 'A very serious situation: Volkswagen could close plants in Germany for the first time in history', CNN Business, [online] nd, Available from: https://www.cnn.com/2024/09/02/investing/volkswagen-factory-closure-germany/index.html [Accessed 3 September 2024].

Colnago, J., Feng, Y., Palanivel, T., Pearman, S., Ung, M., Acquisti, A. et al (2020) 'Informing the design of a personalized privacy assistant for the Internet of Things', in Proceedings of the 2020 CHI Conference on Human Factors in Computing Systems. ACM Press, pp 1–13.

Commission Nationale de l'Informatique et des Libertés (2019) 'Délibération SAN-2019-001 du 21 Janvier 2019', [online] Available from: https://www.legifrance.gouv.fr/cnil/id/CNILTEXT000038032552/ [Accessed 23 February 2023].

Commission Nationale de l'Informatique et des Libertés (2023) 'Advertising ID: Apple Distribution International fined 8 million euros', CNIL, [online] nd, Available from: https://www.cnil.fr/en/advertising-id-apple-distribut ion-international-fined-8-million-euros [Accessed 23 February 2023].

Competition and Markets Authority (2020) 'Online platforms and digital advertising', Available from: https://assets.publishing.service.gov.uk/media/5efc57ed3a6f4023d242ed56/Final_report_1_July_2020_.pdf [Accessed 28 October 2022].

Competition and Markets Authority (2022a) 'CMA's market study into mobile ecosystems: Final report summary', Available from: https://assets.publishing.service.gov.uk/media/62a228228fa8f50395c0a104/Final_rep ort_summary_doc.pdf [Accessed 22 August 2025].

Competition and Markets Authority (2022b) 'Mobile ecosystems market study final report', Available from: https://www.gov.uk/government/publications/mobile-ecosystems-market-study-final-report [Accessed 2 February 2023].

Cook, T. (2020) 'Our Commitment to Human Rights', Available from: https://s203.q4cdn.com/367071867/files/doc_downloads/gov_docs/Apple-Human-Rights-Policy.pdf [Accessed 22 August 2025].

CookiePro (2021) 'CookiePro launches consent rate optimization: Maximize opt-ons and personalize user experiences', CookiePro, [online] nd, Available from: https://www.cookiepro.com/blog/cookiepro-consent-rate-optimization/ [Accessed 28 March 2023].

Court of Justice of the European Union (2016) 'Judgement in Case C-582/14 -Breyer', Available from: https://curia.europa.eu/juris/liste.jsf?num=C-582/14 [Accessed 22 August 2025].

Court of Justice of the European Union (2018) 'Judgement in Case C-210/16 - Wirtschaftsakademie', Available from: https://curia.europa.eu/juris/liste.jsf?num=C-210/16 [Accessed 22 August 2025].

Court of Justice of the European Union (2019) 'Judgement in Case C-40/17 - Fashion ID', Available from: https://curia.europa.eu/juris/liste.jsf?num=C-40/17 [Accessed 22 August 2025].

Court of Justice of the European Union (2020) 'Judgement in Case C-311/18 - Schrems II', Available from: https://curia.europa.eu/juris/liste.jsf?num=C-311/18 [Accessed 22 August 2025].

Datenschutzkonferenz (2019) 'Orientierungshilfe der Aufsichtsbehörden für Anbieter von Telemedien', Available from: https://www.datenschu tzkonferenz-online.de/media/oh/20190405_oh_tmg.pdf [Accessed 22 August 2025].

Datta, S. (2022) 'Cross-reality re-rendering: Manipulating between digital and physical realities', Available from: https://doi.org/10.48550/ arXiv.2211.08005 [Accessed 22 August 2025].

Datta, S., Kollnig, K. and Shadbolt, N. (2022a) 'Greasevision: Rewriting the rules of the interface', in Proceedings of the First Workshop on Dynamic Adversarial Data Collection (DADC 2022). 14 July. Association for Computational Linguistics, pp 7–22.

Datta, S., Kollnig, K. and Shadbolt, N. (2022b) 'Mind-proofing your phone: Navigating the digital minefield with GreaseTerminator', in 27th International Conference on Intelligent User Interfaces. 22–25 March. ACM Press, pp 523–36.

Didomi (2021) 'Consent rate per CMP format', [online] nd, Available from: https://support.didomi.io/consent-rate-per-cmp-format [Accessed 28 March 2023].

Dubé, J.-P., Hitsch, G.J. and Chintagunta, P. (2007) 'Tipping and concentration in markets with indirect network effects', *Marketing Science*, 29(2): 216–49.

Egele, M., Kruegel, C. and Vigna, G. (2011) 'PiOS: Detecting Privacy Leaks in iOS Applications', in *Proceedings of NDSS 2011*.

eMarketer (2022) 'US smartphone in-app purchases to pass $40 billion mark this year', eMarketer, [online] nd, Available from: https://www.emarketer. com/content/us-smartphone-in-app-purchases [Accessed 2 August 2024].

Enck, W., Bilbert, P., Chun, B.-G., Cox, L.P., Jung., J., McDaniel, P. et al (2010) 'TaintDroid: An information-flow tracking system for realtime privacy monitoring on smartphones', in Proceedings of the 9th USENIX Conference on Operating Systems Design and Implementation. (OSDI'10). USENIX, pp 393–407.

European Commission (2016) 'State aid: Irish tax treatment of Apple is illegal', European Commission, Available from: https://ec.europa.eu/com mission/presscorner/detail/en/IP_16_2923 [Accessed 2 February 2023].

European Commission (2020) 'Mergers: Commission clears acquisition of Fitbit by Google, European Commission', European Commission, Available from: https://ec.europa.eu/commission/presscorner/detail/en/ip_20_2 484 [Accessed 11 August 2023].

European Commission (2024) 'Commission opens non-compliance investigations against Alphabet, Apple and Meta under the Digital Markets Act', European Commission, Available from: https://ec.europa.eu/com mission/presscorner/detail/en/ip_24_1689 [Accessed 8 May 2024].

European Data Protection Board (2023) 'Guidelines 03/2022 on Deceptive design patterns in social media platform interfaces: How to recognise and avoid them (Version 2.0)', Available from: https://www.edpb.europa.eu/our-work-tools/our-documents/guidelines/guidelines-032022-deceptive-design-patterns-social-media_en [Accessed 5 May 2025].

ExchangeWire (2024) 'How the DMA is reshaping ad tech for better or worse', ExchangeWire.com, [online] nd, Available from: https://www.exchangewire.com/blog/2024/03/28/how-the-dma-is-reshaping-ad-tech-for-better-or-worse/ [Accessed 9 May 2024].

Eyal, N. and Hoover, R. (2013) *Hooked: How to Build Habit-Forming Products*. Portfolio/Penguin.

Federal Trade Commission (2013) 'Mobile privacy disclosures: Building trust through transparency', [online] nd, Available from: https://www.ftc.gov/sites/default/files/documents/reports/mobile-privacy-disclosures-building-trust-through-transparency-federal-trade-commission-staff-report/130201mobileprivacyreport.pdf [Accessed 13 February 2022].

Felt, A.P., Greenwood, K. and Wagner, D. (2011) 'The effectiveness of application permissions', in Proceedings of the 2nd USENIX Conference on Web Application Development. (WebApps'11). 15–16 June.

Financial Times (2020a) 'Apple commits to freedom of speech after criticism of China censorship', Financial Times, [online] 4 September, Available from: https://www.ft.com/content/a88f5d3d-0102-4616-8b3f-cb0661ba305d [Accessed 28 April 2025].

Financial Times (2020b) 'Combustion engine gains are not exhausted', Financial Times, [online] 11 November, Available from: https://www.ft.com/content/6c202653-fb06-4f4b-9af1-11bb365e9f05 [Accessed 14 July 2023].

Financial Times (2023a) 'Apple's manufacturing shift to India hits stumbling blocks', Financial Times, [online] 14 February, Available from: https://www.ft.com/content/0d70a823-0fba-49ae-a453-2518afcb01f9 [Accessed 26 March 2023].

Financial Times (2023b) 'Tim Cook praises Apple's "symbiotic" relationship with China', Financial Times, [online] 25 March, Available from: https://www.ft.com/content/e5bc3ec2-b522-48c8-880f-7e981c14c9aa [Accessed 26 March 2023].

Financial Times (2023c) 'What it would take for Apple to disentangle itself from China', Financial Times, [online] 18 January, Available from: https://www.ft.com/content/74f7e284-c047-4cc4-9b7a-408d40611bfa [Accessed 26 March 2023].

Financial Times (2024) 'Palantir and Anduril join forces with tech groups to bid for Pentagon contracts', Financial Times, [online] 22 December, Available from: https://www.ft.com/content/6cfdfe2b-6872-4963-bde8-dc6c43be5093 [Accessed 29 December 2024].

First Senate of the Bundesverfassungsgericht (1983) *1 BvR 484/83*, [online] nd, Available from: https://www.bundesverfassungsgericht.de/SharedD ocs/Entscheidungen/EN/1983/12/rs19831215_1bvr020983en.html [Accessed 1 January 2025].

Fuchs, C. (2021) *Social media: A Critical Introduction* (3rd edn). Sage.

Gadgets 360 (2013) 'Samsung's T9000 smart refrigerator runs on Android, includes apps like Evernote and Epicurious', Gadgets 360, [online] Available from: https://www.gadgets360.com/others/news/samsungs-t9000-smart-refrigerator-runs-on-android-includes-apps-like-evernote-and-epicuri ous-320610 [Accessed 3 September 2024].

Gamba, J., Rashed, M., Razaghpanah, A., Tapiador, J. and Vallina-Rodriguex, N. (2020) 'An Analysis of Pre-installed Android Software', in 41st IEEE Symposium on Security and Privacy. 18–20 May. IEEE.

GamesIndustry (2023) 'Report - Sony fails to appeal Austrian loot box verdict', GamesIndustry.biz, [online] nd, Available from: https://www.gamesindustry.biz/report-sony-fails-to-appeal-austrian-loot-box-verdict [Accessed 26 July 2024].

Gao, P., Lee, C. and Murphy, D. (2020) 'Financing dies in darkness? The impact of newspaper closures on public finance', *Journal of Financial Economics*, 135(2): 445–67.

Gegevensbeschermingsautoriteit (2022) 'Decision on complaint relating to Transparency & Consent Framework (case number DOS-2019-01377)', Available from: https://www.gegevensbeschermingsautoriteit.be/publi cations/beslissing-ten-gronde-nr.-21-2022-english.pdf [Accessed 23 February 2023].

Gilens, M. and Page, B.I. (2014) 'Testing theories of American politics: Elites, interest groups, and average citizens', *Perspectives on Politics*, 12(3): 564–81.

Ginsburg, K.R. (2007) 'The importance of play in promoting healthy child development and maintaining strong parent-child bonds', *Pediatrics*, 119(1): 182–91.

Google (2005) 'About the AOL announcement', Official Google Blog, [online] nd, Available from: https://googleblog.blogspot.com/2005/12/about-aol-announcement.html [Accessed 1 June 2023].

Google (2013) 'Google Play Services 4.0', Android Developers Blog, [online] Available from: https://android-developers.googleblog.com/2013/10/goo gle-play-services-40.html [Accessed 23 February 2023].

Google (2015) 'Android – Marshmallow', Android, [online] nd, Available from: https://www.android.com/intl/en_uk/versions/marshmallow-6-0/ [Accessed 23 February 2023].

Google (2022) 'Developer program policy: Play Console Help', [online] 27 July, Available from: https://support.google.com/googleplay/android-developer/answer/12253906?hl=en [Accessed 10 February 2023].

Google (2024) 'Device and network abuse', [online] nd, Available from: https://support.google.com/googleplay/android-developer/answer/9888379 [Accessed 29 December 2024].

Gray, C.M., Kou, Y., Battles, B., Hoggatt, J. and Toombs, A.L. (2018) 'The dark (patterns) side of UX design', in Proceedings of the 2018 CHI Conference on Human Factors in Computing Systems. (CHI '18). ACM Press, pp 1–14.

Greene, D. and Shilton, K. (2018) 'Platform privacies: Governance, collaboration, and the different meanings of "privacy" in iOS and Android development', New Media & Society, 20(4): 1640–57.

Haidt, J. (2024) The Anxious Generation: How the Great Rewiring of Childhood is Causing an Epidemic of Mental Illness. Penguin.

Han, C., Reyes, I., Feal, À., Reardon, J., Wijesekera, P., Vallina-Rodriguez, N. et al (2020) 'The price is (not) right: Comparing privacy in free and paid apps', Proceedings on Privacy Enhancing Technologies, 3: 222–42.

Harkous, H., Fawaz, K., Lebret, R., Schaub, F., Shin, K.G. and Aberer, K. (2018) 'Polisis: Automated analysis and presentation of privacy policies using deep learning', in Proceedings of the 27th USENIX Conference on Security Symposium. (SEC '18). USENIX Association, pp 531–48.

Hey (2024) 'Apple rejects the HEY Calendar from their App Store', [online] nd, Available from: https://world.hey.com/dhh/apple-rejects-the-hey-calendar-from-their-app-store-4316dc03 [Accessed 13 December 2024].

Hoffmann, J., Herrmann, L. and Kestler, L. (2024) 'Gatekeeper's potential privilege: The need to limit DMA centralization', Journal of Antitrust Enforcement, 12(1): 126–47.

Holzer, A. and Ondrus, J. (2011) 'Mobile application market: A developer's perspective', Telematics and Informatics, 28(1): 22–31.

In An Age (2014) 'Gamer demographics over time', In An Age, [blog] Available from: https://inanage.com/2014/10/08/gamer-demographics-over-time/ [Accessed 11 August 2023].

Information Commissioner's Office (2020) 'Age appropriate design: a code of practice for online services', Available from: https://ico.org.uk/for-organi sations/uk-gdpr-guidance-and-resources/childrens-information/childr ens-code-guidance-and-resources/age-appropriate-design-a-code-of-pract ice-for-online-services/ [Accessed 5 May 2025].

Interactive Advertising Bureau (2021) 'Internet Advertising Revenue Report', Available from: https://www.iab.com/insights/internet-advertis ing-revenue-report/ [Accessed 25 August 2025].

International Consortium of Investigative Journalists (2022) ' "Delaware is everywhere": How a little-known tax haven made the rules for corporate America', [online] Available from: https://www.icij.org/inside-icij/2022/06/delaware-is-everywhere-how-a-little-known-tax-haven-made-the-rules-for-corporate-america/ [Accessed 7 May 2024].

Iqbal, U., Bahrami, P.N., Trimananda, R., Cui, H., Gamero-Garrido, A., Dubois, D.J. et al (2023) 'Tracking, profiling, and ad targeting in the Alexa Echo smart speaker ecosystem', in Proceedings of the 2023 ACM on Internet Measurement Conference. (IMC '23). 24–26 October. ACM Press, pp 569–83.

Irish Council for Civil Liberties (2021) 'Europe's enforcement paralysis: ICCL's 2021 report on the enforcement capacity of data protection authorities', ICCL, Available from: https://www.iccl.ie/digital-data/2021-gdpr-rep ort/ [Accessed 26 September 2021].

James, L. (2021) 'These are the latest developments on the chip shortage in 2021', Available from: https://www.power-and-beyond.com/update-these-are-the-latest-developments-on-the-chip-shortage-in-2021-a-a259c f333ff4ecd243eb491337757493/ [Accessed 13 July 2023].

Jobs, S. (2010) 'Thoughts on flash', Available from: https://web.archive.org/ web/20150715043545/https://www.apple.com/hotnews/thoughts-on-flash/ [Accessed 18 December 2024].

J.P. Morgan (2023) 'Supply chain issues and autos: When will the chip shortage end?', Available from: https://www.jpmorgan.com/insights/current-events/ supply-chain/supply-chain-chip-shortage [Accessed 13 July 2023].

Kelley, P.G., Bresee, J., Cranor, L.F. and Reeder, R.W. (2009) 'A "nutrition label" for privacy', in Proceedings of the 5th Symposium on Usable Privacy and Security. (SOUPS '09). 15–17 July. ACM Press, p 1.

Kelley, P.G., Cranor, L.F. and Sadeh, N. (2013) 'Privacy as part of the app decision-making process', in Proceedings of the SIGCHI Conference on Human Factors in Computing Systems. (CHI '13). ACM Press, p 3393.

Kokott, J. and Sobotta, C. (2013) 'The distinction between privacy and data protection in the jurisprudence of the CJEU and the ECtHR', *International Data Privacy Law*, 3(4): 222–8.

Kollnig, K. (2023) 'Regulatory technologies for the study of data and platform power in the app economy'. PhD Thesis. University of Oxford, Available from: https://kollnig.net/phd-thesis [Accessed 19 May 2023].

Kollnig, K. and Bolt, N. (2022) 'TrackerControl: Transparency and choice around app tracking', *Journal of Open Source Software*, 7(75): 4270.

Kollnig, K. and Dewitte, P. (2023) '"GDPR compliance is hard", but is it? – 20 hours to overcome privacy issues in mobile apps', *Internet Policy Review*, Available from: https://policyreview.info/articles/news/gdpr-com pliance-privacy-issues-mobile-apps/1678 [Accessed 28 August 2023].

Kollnig, K. and Shadolt, N. (2023) 'How Decisions by Apple and Google obstruct App Privacy', *Technology and Regulation*, Available from: https:// doi.org/10.26116/techreg.2023.002 [Accessed 1 February 2023].

Kollnig, K., Datta, S. and Van Kleek, M. (2021) 'I want my app that way: Reclaiming sovereignty over personal devices', in Extended Abstracts of the 2021 CHI Conference on Human Factors in Computing Systems. (CHI EA '21). ACM Press, pp 1–8.

Kollnig, K., Binns, R., Dewitte, P., Van Kleek, M., Wang, G., Omeiza, D.N. et al (2021a) 'A fait accompli? An empirical study into the absence of consent to third-party tracking in Android Apps', in Proceedings of the Seventeenth Symposium on Usable Privacy and Security. 8–10 August. USENIX, p 16, Available from: https://www.usenix.org/system/files/soups2021-kollnig.pdf [Accessed 19 May 2023].

Kollnig, K., Binns, R., Van Kleek, M., Lyngs, U., Zhao, J., Tinsman, C. et al (2021b) 'Before and after GDPR: Tracking in mobile apps', *Internet Policy Review*, 10(4).

Kollnig, K., Shuba, A., Binns, R., Van Kleek, M. and Shadbolt, N. (2022a) 'Are iPhones really better for privacy? A comparative study of iOS and Android apps', *Proceedings on Privacy Enhancing Technologies*, 2022(2): 6–24.

Kollnig, K., Shuba, A., Van Kleek, M., Binns, R. and Shadbolt, N. (2022b) 'Goodbye tracking? Impact of iOS app tracking transparency and privacy labels', in 2022 ACM Conference on Fairness, Accountability, and Transparency. (FAccT '22). ACM Press, pp 508–20.

Kollnig, K., Datta, S., Serban Von Davier, T., Van Kleek, M., Binns, R., Lyngs, U. et al (2023) ' "We are adults and deserve control of our phones": Examining the risks and opportunities of a right to repair for mobile apps', in Proceedings of the 2023 ACM Conference on Fairness, Accountability, and Transparency. 12–15 June. ACM Press, pp 22–34.

Landemore, H. (2021) 'Open democracy and digital technologies', in L. Bernholz, H. Landemore, and R. Reich (eds) *Digital Technology and Democratic Theory*. University of Chicago Press, pp 62–89.

Laperdrix, P., Mehanna, N., Durey, A. and Rudametkin, W. (2022) 'The price to play: A privacy analysis of free and paid games in the android ecosystem', in Proceedings of the ACM Web Conference 2022. (WWW '22). 25–29 April. ACM Press, pp 3440–9.

Le, A., Varmarken, J., Langhoff, S., Shuba., A., Gjoka, M. and Markopoulou, A. (2015) 'AntMonitor: A system for monitoring from mobile devices', in Proceedings of the 2015 ACM SIGCOMM Workshop on Crowdsourcing and Crowdsharing of Big (Internet) Data. (C2B(1)D '15). ACM Press, pp 15–20.

Leith, D.J. (2021) 'Mobile handset privacy: Measuring the data iOS and Android send to Apple and Google', in *SecureComm 2021*. Springer, p 10.

Leprince-Ringuet, D. (2020) 'Contact-tracing app: How did the UK go so badly wrong?', ZDNET, Available from: https://www.zdnet.com/article/contact-tracing-app-how-did-the-uk-go-so-badly-wrong/ [Accessed 21 November 2022].

Lero, T. (2022) ' "Il faudra s'en souvenir": Cédric O règle ses comptes avec Apple', *BFM BUSINESS*, Available from: https://www.bfmtv.com/economie/entreprises/services/il-faudra-s-en-souvenir-cedric-o-regle-ses-comptes-avec-apple_AV-202005050292.html [Accessed 21 November 2022].

Lessig, L. (2006) *Code 2.0* (1st edn). Basic Books.

Li, T., Reiman, K., Argawal, Y., Cranor, L.F. and Hong, J.I. (2022) 'Understanding challenges for developers to create accurate privacy nutrition labels', in CHI Conference on Human Factors in Computing Systems. 30 April–5 May. ACM Press, pp 1–24.

Li, Z., Nan, G. and Li, M. (2020) 'Effects of platform protection in a duopoly in the presence of asymmetric information and user security preference', *SSRN Electronic Journal*, Available from: https://www.doi.org/10.2139/ssrn.3556488 [Accessed 21 November 2022].

Liu, H., Leith, D.J. and Patras, P. (2023) 'Android OS privacy under the Loupe: A Tale from the East', Available from: https://www.doi.org/10.48550/arXiv.2302.01890 [Accessed 21 November 2022].

Lyngs, U., Lukoff, K., Slovak, P., Seymour, W., Webb, H., Jirotka, M. et al (2020) '"I just want to hack myself to not get distracted": Evaluating design interventions for self-control on Facebook', in Proceedings of the 2020 CHI Conference on Human Factors in Computing Systems. 25–30 April. ACM Press, pp 1–15.

Lynskey, O. (2015) *The Foundations of EU Data Protection Law* (1st edn). Oxford University Press.

Massé, E. (2020) 'Two years under GDPR: An implementation progress report', *Access Now*, Available from: https://www.accessnow.org/cms/assets/uploads/2020/05/Two-Years-Under-GDPR.pdf [Accessed 21 November 2022].

Matte, C., Bielova, N. and Santos, C. (2019) 'Do cookie banners respect my choice? Measuring legal compliance of banners from IAB Europe's transparency and consent framework', Available from: http://arxiv.org/abs/1911.09964 [Accessed 14 February 2020].

Mazzucato, M. (2018) *The Entrepreneurial State: Debunking Public vs. Private Sector Myths*. Penguin.

McDonald, A.M. and Cranor, L.F. (2008) 'The cost of reading privacy policies', *I/S: A Journal of Law and Policy for the Information Society*, 4(3): 26.

Mhaidli, A.H., Zou, Y. and Schaub, F. (2019) '"We can't live without them!" App developers' adoption of ad networks and their considerations of consumer risks', in Proceedings of the Fifteenth Symposium on Usable Privacy and Security. 12–13 August. USENIX, p 21.

microg (nd) 'Implementation status', GitHub, [online] nd, Available from: https://github.com/microg/GmsCore [Accessed 29 December 2024].

Morton, F.S., Dinielli, D., Cooper, A., Kimmelman, G. and O'Grady, M. (2024) 'Judicial remedies to restore lost competition in the market for general search', Available from: https://tobin.yale.edu/sites/default/files/publication-documents/2024-09/Judicial%20Remedies%20To%20Restore%20Lost%20Competition%20in%20the%20Market%20for%20General%20Search-for%20posting.pdf [Accessed 20 December 2024].

Munir, S., Kollnig, K., Shuba, A. and Shafiq, Z. (2024) 'Google's Chrome antitrust paradox', *Vanderbilt Journal of Entertainment & Technology Law*, 27, Available from: https://papers.ssrn.com/abstract=4780718 [Accessed 25 April 2024].

Netzpolitik (2022) 'Privacy labels fail: Many "tracking-free" apps in iOS secretly track users', netzpolitik.org, [online] nd, Available from: https://netzpolitik.org/2022/privacy-labels-fail-many-tracking-free-apps-in-ios-secretly-track-users/ [Accessed 29 March 2023].

Nissenbaum, H. (2004) 'Privacy as contextual integrity', *Washington Law Review*, 79: 39.

Norval, C., Janssen, H., Cobbe, J. and Singh, J. (2018) 'Reclaimimg data: Overcoming app identification barriers for exercising data protection rights', in Proceedings of the 2018 ACM International Joint Conference and 2018 International Symposium on Pervasive and Ubiquitous Computing and Wearable Computers. (UbiComp '18). ACM Press, pp 921–30.

Norwegian Consumer Council (2020) 'Out of control: How consumers are exploited by the online advertising industry', Available from: https://fil.for brukerradet.no/wp-content/uploads/2020/01/2020-01-14-out-of-cont rol-final-version.pdf [Accessed 4 May 2024].

Nouwens, M., Liccardi, I., Veale, M., Karger, D. and Kagal, L. (2020) 'Dark patterns after the GDPR: Scraping consent pop-ups and demonstrating their influence', Proceedings of the 2020 CHI Conference on Human Factors in Computing Systems. 25–30 April, Available from: https//www.doi.org/10.1145/3313831.3376321 [Accessed 4 May 2024].

NPR (2021) 'Singapore says COVID-19 contact-tracing data can be requested by police', NPR, [online] 5 January, Available from: https://www.npr.org/sections/coronavirus-live-updates/2021/01/05/953604553/singapore-says-covid-19-contact-tracing-data-can-be-requested-by-police [Accessed 4 May 2025].

OECD (2023) 'International tax reform: OECD releases technical guidance for implementation of the global minimum tax', *OECD*, Available from: https://www.oecd.org/tax/beps/international-tax-reform-oecd-releases-technical-guidance-for-implementation-of-the-global-minimum-tax.htm [Accessed 7 May 2024].

Ó Fathaigh, R. and van Hoboken, J. (2019) 'European regulation of smartphone ecosystems', *European Data Protection Law Review*, 5(4): 476–91.

Ó Fathaigh, R., van Hoboken, J. and Van Eijk, N. (2018) 'Mobile privacy and business-to-platform dependencies: An analysis of SEC disclosures', *Journal of Business and Technology Law*, 14(1): 49–105.

Okoyomon, E., Samarin, N., Wijesekera, P., Elazari, A., Vallina-Rodriguez, N., Reyes, I. et al (2019) 'On the ridiculousness of notice and consent: Contradictions in app privacy policies', in The Workshop on Technology and Consumer Protection. (ConPro '19). 23 May.

Pew Research Center (2019) 'Americans and privacy: Concerned, confused and feeling lack of control over their personal information', Pew Research Center, Available from: https://www.pewresearch.org/internet/2019/11/15/americans-and-privacy-concerned-confused-and-feeling-lack-of-control-over-their-personal-information/ [Accessed 28 March 2023].

Poell, T., Nieborg, D.B. and Duffy, B.E. (2022) *Platforms and Cultural Production*. Polity Press.

Portuese, A. (2021) 'The Digital Markets Act: European precautionary antitrust', *Information Technology & Innovation Foundation*, Available from: https://itif.org/publications/2021/05/24/digital-markets-act-european-precautionary-antitrust/ [Accessed 9 May 2024].

Public Citizen (2022) 'Lobby, donate, hire, repeat', Public Citizen, Available from: https://www.citizen.org/article/lobby-donate-hire-repeat/ [Accessed 8 May 2024].

Reardon, J., Feal, À., Wijesekera, P., On, A.E.B., Vallina-Rodriguez, N. and Egelman, S. (2019) '50 ways to leak your data: An exploration of apps' circumvention of the Android Permissions System', in 28th USENIX security symposium (USENIX security 2019), 14–16 August. USENIX Association, pp 603–20, Available from: https://www.usenix.org/conference/usenixsecurity19/presentation/reardon [Accessed 8 May 2024].

Recruitonomics (2023) 'The decline of car manufacturing is hurting the German economy', Recruitonomics, [online] nd, Available from: https://recruitonomics.com/the-decline-of-car-manufacturing-is-hurting-the-german-economy/ [Accessed 13 July 2023].

Reidenberg, J.R., Bhatia, J., Breaux, T.D. and Norton, T.B. (2016) 'Ambiguity in privacy policies and the impact of regulation', *The Journal of Legal Studies*, 45(S2): S163–90.

Ren, J., Rao, A., Lindorfer, M., Legout, A. and Chorrnes, D. (2016) 'ReCon: Revealing and controlling PII leaks in mobile network traffic', in Proceedings of the 14th Annual International Conference on Mobile Systems, Applications, and Services. (MobiSys '16). 26–30 June. ACM Press, pp 361–74.

Reuters (2017) 'EU lost up to 5.4 billion euros in tax revenues from Google, Facebook', *Reuters*, [online] 13 September, Available from: https://www.reuters.com/article/us-eu-tax-digital-idUSKCN1BO226 [Accessed 26 March 2023].

Reuters (2018) 'UN investigators cite Facebook role in Myanmar crisis', *Reuters*, [online] 12 March, Available from: https://www.reuters.com/article/us-myanmar-rohingya-facebook-idUKKCN1GO2PN [Accessed 23 February 2023].

Reuters (2021) 'Israeli Supreme Court bans unlimited COVID-19 mobile phone tracking', *Reuters*, [online] 1 March, Available from: https://www.reuters.com/article/world/israeli-supreme-court-bans-unlimited-covid-19-mobile-phone-tracking-idUSKCN2AT25Q/ [Accessed 4 May 2025].

Reuters (2022) 'China bank protest stopped by health codes turning red, depositors say', *Reuters*, [online] 16 June, Available from: https://www.reuters.com/world/china/china-bank-protest-stopped-by-health-codes-turning-red-depositors-say-2022-06-14/ [Accessed 4 May 2025].

Reuters (2024a) 'Apple pulls WhatsApp, Threads from China app store after Beijing order', *Reuters*, [online] 19 April, Available from: https://www.reuters.com/technology/apple-removes-whatsapp-threads-china-app-store-wsj-reports-2024-04-19/ [Accessed 2 August 2024].

Reuters (2024b) 'Exclusive: EU's new tech laws are working: small browsers gain market share', *Reuters*, [online] 10 April, Available from: https://www.reuters.com/technology/eus-new-tech-laws-are-working-small-browsers-gain-market-share-2024-04-10/ [Accessed 8 May 2024].

Reuters (2024c) 'How drone combat in Ukraine is changing warfare', *Reuters*, [online] 26 March, Available from: https://www.reuters.com/graphics/UKRAINE-CRISIS/DRONES/dwpkeyjwkpm/ [Accessed 1 January 2025].

Reuters (2024d) 'US prosecutors demand Google divest Chrome to end search monopoly', *Reuters*, [online] 21 November, Available from: https://www.reuters.com/technology/us-prosecutors-demand-google-divest-chrome-end-search-monopoly-2024-11-21/ [Accessed 20 December 2024].

Reuters (2025) 'Apple moving to make most iPhones for US in India rather than China, source says', *Reuters*, [online] 25 April, Available from: https://www.reuters.com/world/china/apple-aims-source-all-us-iphones-india-pivot-away-china-ft-reports-2025-04-25/ [Accessed 28 April 2025].

Reyes, I., Wijesekera, P., Reardon, J., On, A.E.B., Razaghpanah, A., Vallina-Rodriguez, N. and Egelman, S. (2018) '"Won't somebody think of the children?" Examining COPPA compliance at scale', *Proceedings on Privacy Enhancing Technologies*, 2018(3): 63–83.

Roma, P. and Ragaglia, D. (2016) 'Revenue models, in-app purchase, and the app performance: Evidence from Apple's App Store and Google Play', *Electronic Commerce Research and Applications*, 17: 173–90.

Roşca, C. (2024) *Digital Arms for Digital Consumer Harms: Mapping Legal and Technical Solutions for Dark Patterns in EU Consumer Law*. Maastricht University Press.

ScreenRant (2022) 'The "spirit of the iPod" lives on in the Apple Watch', ScreenRant, [online] nd, Available from: https://screenrant.com/apple-watch-ipod-natural-evolution-successor-why/ [Accessed 3 September 2024].

Sharon, T. (2020) 'Blind-sided by privacy? Digital contact tracing, the Apple/Google API and big tech's newfound role as global health policy makers', *Ethics and Information Technology*, 23(1): 45–57.

Sharon, T. (2023) 'Sphere transgressions by tech giants', [online] Available from: https://conference.publicspaces.net/en/session/keynote-bu [Accessed 29 March 2023].

Shklovski, I., Mainwaring, S.D., Skúladóttir, H.H. and Borgthorsson, H. (2014) 'Leakiness and creepiness in app space: Perceptions of privacy and mobile app use', in Proceedings of the 32nd Annual ACM Conference on Human Factors in Computing Systems. (CHI '14). 26 April–1 May. ACM Press, pp 2347–56.

Shuba, A., Markopoulou, A. and Shafiq, Z. (2018) 'NoMoAds: Effective and efficient cross-app mobile ad-blocking', *Proceedings on Privacy Enhancing Technologies*, 2018(4): 125–40.

SlashGear (2020) 'Google SafetyNet update might be the end for Android rooting, custom ROMs', SlashGear, [online] nd, Available from: https://www.slashgear.com/google-safetynet-update-might-be-the-end-for-android-rooting-custom-roms-01627121/ [Accessed 24 October 2022].

Slate (2021) 'A prominent priest was outed for using Grindr: Experts say it's a warning sign', Slate, [online] nd, Available from: https://slate.com/technology/2021/07/catholic-priest-grindr-data-privacy.html [Accessed 28 March 2023].

Srnicek, N. (2016) *Platform Capitalism*. Polity Press.

Solove, D.J. (2012) 'Privacy self-management and the consent dilemma', *Social Science Research Network*, Available from: https://papers.ssrn.com/abstract=2171018 [Accessed 13 February 2020].

Standing, G. (2016) 'Meet the precariat, the new global class fuelling the rise of populism', *World Economic Forum*, Available from: https://www.weforum.org/agenda/2016/11/precariat-global-class-rise-of-populism/ [Accessed 29 March 2023].

Statista (2021a) 'Infographic: Mobile gaming: Just a quick fix', Statista Daily Data, [online] nd, Available from: https://www.statista.com/chart/26324/average-time-per-day-spent-on-mobile-games-on-android [Accessed 26 July 2024].

Statista (2021b) 'Number of mobile gamers worldwide by region 2021', Statista, [online] nd, Available from: https://www.statista.com/statistics/512112/number-mobile-gamers-world-by-region/ [Accessed 11 August 2023].

Statista (2022a) 'Facebook users reach by device 2022', Statista, [online] nd, Available from: https://www.statista.com/statistics/377808/distribution-of-facebook-users-by-device/ [Accessed 2 February 2023].

Statista (2022b) 'Infographic: Apple several ticks ahead in the smartwatch market', Statista Daily Data, [online] nd, Available from: https://www.statista.com/chart/15035/worldwide-smartwatch-shipments [Accessed 3 September 2024].

Statista (2022c) 'Infographic: Texting is alive and well at 30', Statista Daily Data, [online] nd, Available from: https://www.statista.com/chart/12109/sms-volume-in-the-united-states [Accessed 10 August 2023].

Statista (2023a) 'Distribution of free and paid Android apps 2023', Statista, [online] nd, Available from: https://www.statista.com/statistics/266211/distribution-of-free-and-paid-android-apps/ [Accessed 31 May 2023].

Statista (2023b) 'Distribution of free and paid iOS apps 2023', Statista, [online] nd, Available from: https://www.statista.com/statistics/1020996/distribution-of-free-and-paid-ios-apps/ [Accessed 31 May 2023].

Statista (2023c) 'Duolingo Inc. quarterly revenue 2023', Statista, [online] nd, Available from: https://www.statista.com/statistics/1247811/quarterly-duolingo-revenue/ [Accessed 11 August 2023].

Statista (2023d) 'Infographic: Games dominate global app revenue', Statista Daily Data, [online] nd, Available from: https://www.statista.com/chart/29389/global-app-revenue-by-segment [Accessed 11 August 2023].

Statista (2023e) 'Infographic: Google remains a niche player in the smartphone market', Statista Daily Data, [online] nd, Available from: https://www.statista.com/chart/25463/popularity-of-google-smartphones [Accessed 25 October 2023].

Statista (2024) 'Smartphone subscriptions worldwide 2027', Statista, [online] nd, Available from: https://www.statista.com/statistics/330695/number-of-smartphone-users-worldwide/ [Accessed 26 March 2023].

Takahashi, D. (2014) 'Only 0.15 percent of mobile gamers account for 50 percent of all in-game revenue (exclusive)', *VentureBeat*, Available from: https://venturebeat.com/business/only-0-15-of-mobile-gamers-account-for-50-percent-of-all-in-game-revenue-exclusive/ [Accessed 11 August 2023].

Taylor Wessing (2022) ' "ICO says future of "Real Time Bidding" in Adtech "is in the balance"', Available from: https://www.taylorwessing.com/en/insights-and-events/insights/2020/02/ico-says-future-of-real-time-bidding-in-adtech-is-in-the-balance [Accessed 9 August 2024].

TechCrunch (2019) 'Apple restricts ads and third-party trackers in iPhone apps for kids', TechCrunch, [online] nd, Available from: https://techcrunch.com/2019/06/03/apple-kid-apps-trackers/ [Accessed 29 March 2023].

TechCrunch (2020a) 'Apple CEO Tim Cook questioned over App Store's removal of rival screen time apps in antitrust hearing', TechCrunch, [online] nd, Available from: https://techcrunch.com/2020/07/29/apple-ceo-tim-cook-questioned-over-app-stores-removal-of-rival-screen-time-apps-in-antitrust-hearing/ [Accessed 2 August 2024].

TechCrunch (2020b) 'Germany ditches centralized approach to app for COVID-19 contacts tracing', TechCrunch, [online] nd, Available from: https://techcrunch.com/2020/04/27/germany-ditches-centralized-approach-to-app-for-covid-19-contacts-tracing/ [Accessed 2 February 2023].

TechCrunch (2021a) 'Apple finally launches a Screen Time API for app developers', TechCrunch, [online] nd, Available from: https://techcrunch.com/2021/06/07/apple-finally-launches-a-screen-time-api-for-app-developers/ [Accessed 2 August 2024].

TechCrunch (2021b) 'Headspace and Ginger are merging to form Headspace Health', TechCrunch, [online] nd, Available from: https://techcrunch.com/2021/08/25/headspace-and-ginger-are-merging-to-form-headspace-health/ [Accessed 11 August 2023].

TechRadar (2008) 'A complete history of Android', TechRadar, [online] nd, Available from: https://www.techradar.com/news/phone-and-communications/mobile-phones/a-complete-history-of-android-470327 [Accessed 9 February 2023].

The Guardian (2020) 'Covidsafe app is not working properly on iPhones, authorities admit', The Guardian, [online] 6 May, Available from: https://www.theguardian.com/world/2020/may/06/covidsafe-app-is-not-working-properly-on-iphones-authorities-admit [Accessed 2 February 2023].

The Nation (2023) 'Lessons from the catastrophic failure of the metaverse', The Nation, Available from: https://www.thenation.com/article/culture/metaverse-zuckerberg-pr-hype/ [Accessed 3 September 2024].

The New York Times (2010) 'Publishers question Apple's rejection of nudity', The New York Times, [online] 15 March, Available from: https://www.nytimes.com/2010/03/15/technology/15cache.html [Accessed 11 February 2023].

The New York Times (2019) 'Apple cracks down on apps that fight iPhone addiction', The New York Times, [online] 27 April, Available from: https://www.nytimes.com/2019/04/27/technology/apple-screen-time-trackers.html [Accessed 11 February 2023].

The New York Times (2022) 'Opinion: I was the head of trust and safety at Twitter – This is what could become of it', The New York Times, [online] 18 November, Available from: https://www.nytimes.com/2022/11/18/opinion/twitter-yoel-roth-elon-musk.html [Accessed 11 February 2023].

The Next Web (2012) 'Steve Jobs speech in 1983 reveals Apple working on iPad for 27 years', The Next Web, [online] nd, Available from: https://thenextweb.com/news/rare-full-recording-of-1983-steve-jobs-speech-reveals-apple-had-been-working-on-ipad-for-27-years [Accessed 3 September 2024].

The Verge (2018) 'Google app suite costs as much as $40 per phone under new EU Android deal', The Verge, [online] nd, Available from: https://www.theverge.com/2018/10/19/17999366/google-eu-android-licensing-terms [Accessed 2 May 2025].

The Verge (2024a) 'Google apologizes for "missing the mark" after Gemini generated racially diverse Nazis', The Verge, [online] nd, Available from: https://www.theverge.com/2024/2/21/24079371/google-ai-gemini-generative-inaccurate-historical [Accessed 26 July 2024].

The Verge (2024b) 'Google scrambles to manually remove weird AI answers in search', The Verge, [online] nd, Available from: https://www.theverge.com/2024/5/24/24164119/google-ai-overview-mistakes-search-race-openai [Accessed 26 July 2024].

Time (2022) 'Schumer kills bills big tech feared most, but boosts budgets of agencies targeting them', Time, Available from: https://time.com/6243256/schumer-kills-antitrust-big-tech-bills/ [Accessed 24 October 2023].

United Nations (2024) 'Global e-waste monitor 2024: Electronic waste rising five times faster than documented e-waste recycling', United Nations Institute for Training and Research, Available from: https://unitar.org/about/news-stories/press/global-e-waste-monitor-2024-electronic-waste-rising-five-times-faster-documented-e-waste-recycling [Accessed 28 December 2024].

van Hoboken, J. and Ó Fathaigh, R. (2021) 'Smartphone platforms as privacy regulators', *Computer Law & Security Review*, 41: 105557.

Van Kleek, M., Binns, R., Zhao, J., Slack, A., Lee, S., Ottewell, et al (2018) 'X-Ray refine: Supporting the exploration and refinement of information exposure resulting from smartphone apps', in Proceedings of the 2018 CHI Conference on Human Factors in Computing Systems. (CHI '18). 21–26 April. ACM Press, pp 1–13.

Veale, M., Binns, R. and Ausloos, J. (2018) 'When data protection by design and data subject rights clash', *International Data Privacy Law*, 8(2):105–23.

Veale, M., Nouwens, M. and Santos, C. (2022) 'Impossible Asks: Can the Transparency and Consent Framework Ever Authorise Real-Time Bidding After the Belgian DPA Decision?' Preprint, Available from: https://www.doi.org/10.31235/osf.io/mj7xu [Accessed 11 August 2023].

VentureBeat (2021) 'Newzoo: Mobile gaming accounts for the largest part of the 2021 market', VentureBeat, Available from: https://venturebeat.com/games/newzoo-mobile-gaming-accounts-for-the-largest-part-of-the-2021-market/ [Accessed 11 August 2023].

Viennot, N., Garcia, E. and Nieh, J. (2014) 'A measurement study of Google Play', in The 2014 ACM International Conference on Measurement and Modeling of Computer Systems. (SIGMETRICS '14). 16–20 June. ACM Press, pp 221–33.

Vines, P., Roesner, F. and Kohno, T. (2017) 'Exploring ADINT: Using ad targeting for surveillance on a budget – or – How Alice can buy ads to track Bob', in Proceedings of the 2017 Workshop on Privacy in the Electronic Society. (WPES '17). 30 October. ACM Press, pp 153–64.

Wachter, S. (2019a) 'Affinity profiling and discrimination by association in online behavioural advertising', *Berkeley Technology Law Journal*, 35(2), Available at https://ssrn.com/abstract=3388639 [Accessed 7 May 2024].

Wachter, S. (2019b) 'Data protection in the age of big data', *Nature Electronics*, 2: 6–7.

Wang, G. (2021) 'Protection or punishment? Relating the design space of parental control spps and perceptions about them to support parenting for online safety', in Proceedings of the ACM on Human-Computer Interaction. (CSCW2). ACM Press, pp 1–26.

Washington Post (2016) 'How the US became one of the world's biggest tax havens', Washington Post, [online] nd, Available from: https://www.was hingtonpost.com/news/wonk/wp/2016/04/05/how-the-u-s-became-one-of-the-worlds-biggest-tax-havens/ [Accessed 7 May 2024].

Washington Post (2022) 'Your kids' apps are spying on them', Washington Post, [online] 9 June, Available from: https://www.washingtonpost.com/technology/2022/06/09/apps-kids-privacy/ [Accessed 29 March 2023].

Washington Post (2023) 'Catholic group spent millions on app data that tracked gay priests', Washington Post, [online] 12 March, Available from: https://www.washingtonpost.com/dc-md-va/2023/03/09/catholics-gay-priests-grindr-data-bishops/ [Accessed 28 March 2023].

Windows Central (2023) 'Microsoft used a factory in Puerto Rico to sidestep $29 billion in taxes, says IRS', Yahoo Finance, Available from: https://finance.yahoo.com/news/microsoft-used-factory-puerto-rico-123631061.html [Accessed 23 October 2023].

World Health Organization (2023) Global Health Expenditure Database, Available from: https://apps.who.int/nha/database [Accessed 11 August 2023].

Wu, T. (2018) *The Curse of Bigness: Antitrust in the New Gilded Age*. Columbia Global Reports.

Xiao, L.Y. (2020) 'People's Republic of China legal update: The notice on the prevention of online gaming addiction in juveniles', *Gaming Law Review*, 24(1): 51–3.

Xiao, L.Y. (2023) 'Breaking ban: Belgium's ineffective gambling law regulation of video game loot boxes', *Collabra: Psychology*, 9(1): 57641.

Zimmeck, S., Story, P., Mullen, D., Ravichander, A., Wang, Z., Reidenberg, J. et al (2019) 'MAPS: Scaling privacy compliance analysis to a million apps', *Proceedings on Privacy Enhancing Technologies*, 2019(3): 66–86.

Zimmeck, S., Aggarwal, N., Lui, Z. and Kollnig, K. (2024) 'From ad identifiers to global privacy control: The status quo and future of opting out of ad tracking on Android', Available from: https://arxiv.org/html/2407.14938v1 [Accessed 11 August 2023].

Zuboff, S. (2019) *The Age of Surveillance Capitalism: The Fight for a Human Future at the New Frontier of Power* (1st edn). PublicAffairs.

Index